2

8

MACMILLAN MODERN NOVELISTS

General Editor: Norman Page

MACMILLAN MODERN NOVELISTS

MACMILLAN MODERN NOVELISTS
TONI MORRISON

Linden Peach

MACMILLAN

First published 1995 by
MACMILLAN PRESS LTD
Houndmills, Basingstoke, Hampshire RG21 2XS
and London
Companies and representatives
throughout the world

ISBN 0–333–62243–X hardcover
ISBN 0–333–62244–8 paperback

A catalogue record for this book is available
from the British Library.

10 9 8 7 6 5 4 3 2 1
04 03 02 01 00 99 98 97 96 95

Printed in Malaysia

Series Standing Order

If you would like to receive future titles in this series as they are
published, you can make use of our standing order facility. To place a
standing order please contact your bookseller or, in case of difficulty,
write to us at the address below with your name and address and the
name of the series. Please state with which title you wish to begin your
standing order. (If you live outside the United Kingdom we may not
have the rights for your area, in which case we will forward your order
to the publisher concerned.)

Customer Services Department, Macmillan Distribution Ltd
Houndmills, Basingstoke, Hampshire, RG21 2XS, England.

Contents

Acknowledgements

I should like to acknowledge a general debt to my colleagues and students in the School of English, Bretton Hall College, University of Leeds, for helping me to refine my ideas. Special thanks are also due to the staff of the library at Bretton Hall for their speedy and efficient assistance. I owe special debts to Angela Burton for her advice and constant encouragement and to Vicky Annand, Goldsmiths' College, University of London, for her painstaking attention to the various drafts. Without their help this book would not have been completed.

General Editor's Preface

The death of the novel has often been announced, and part of the secret of its obstinate vitality must be its capacity for growth, adaptation, self-renewal and self-transformation: like some vigorous organism in a speeded-up Darwinian ecosystem, it adapts itself quickly to a changing world. War and revolution, economic crisis and social change, radically new ideologies such as Marxism and Freudianism, have made this century unprecedented in human history in the speed and extent of change, but the novel has shown an extraordinary capacity to find new forms and techniques and to accommodate new ideas and conceptions of human nature and human experience, and even to take up new positions on the nature of fiction itself.

In the generations immediately preceding and following 1914, the novel underwent a radical redefinition of its nature and possibilities. The present series of monographs is devoted to the novelists who created the modern novel and to those who, in their turn, either continued and extended, or reacted against and rejected, the traditions established during that period of intense exploration and experiment. It includes a number of those who lived and wrote in the nineteenth century but whose innovative contribution to the art of fiction makes it impossible to ignore them in any account of the origins of the modern novel; it also includes the so-called 'modernists' and those who in the mid- and late twentieth century have emerged as outstanding practitioners of this genre. The scope is, inevitably, international; not only, in the migratory and exile-haunted world of our century, do writers refuse to heed national frontiers – 'English' literature lays claim to Conrad the Pole, Henry James the American, and Joyce the Irishman – but geniuses such as Flaubert, Dostoevsky and Kafka have had an influence on the fiction of many nations.

Each volume in the series is intended to provide an introduction to the fiction of the writer concerned, both for those approaching him or her for the first time and for those who are already familiar with some parts of the achievement in question and now wish to place it in the context of the total *œuvre*. Although essential information relating to the writer's life and times is given, usually in an opening chapter, the approach is primarily critical and the emphasis is not upon 'background' or generalisations but upon close examination of important texts. Where an author is notably prolific, major texts have been made to convey, more summarily, a sense of the nature and quality of the author's work as a whole. Those who want to read further will find suggestions in the select bibliography included in each volume. Many novelists are, of course, not only novelists but also poets, essayists, biographers, dramatists, travel writers and so forth; many have practised shorter forms of fiction; and many have written letters or kept diaries that constitute a significant part of their literary output. A brief study cannot hope to deal with all these in detail, but where the shorter fiction and the non-fictional writings, public and private, have an important relationship to the novels, some space has been devoted to them.

NORMAN PAGE

1
Introduction

The black literary tradition now demands, for sustenance and for growth, the sorts of reading which it is the especial province of the literary critic to render; and these sorts of reading all share a fundamental concern with the nature and functions of figurative language as manifested in specific texts. No matter to what ends we put our readings, we can never lose sight of the fact that a text is not a fixed 'thing' but a rhetorical structure which functions in response to a complex set of rules. It can never be related satisfactorily to a reality outside itself merely in a one-to-one relation. (Henry Louis Gates, Jr, 1984, 5)

I

This study of the novels of Toni Morrison, the first African-American writer to win the Nobel Prize for Literature, is aimed at the general reader and the student alike. The intention has been to provide an introduction to the novels which respects both their specificity and the ways in which they relate to each other. In keeping with the overall aims of the series, the discussion of each novel is oriented towards its innovative contribution to the art of fiction. Therefore, the emphasis throughout falls upon each text as a 'rhetorical structure' which extends or challenges what readers might expect of a novel. Yet because Toni Morrison is an African-American author whose works have their origins in the tense interface between a number of cultures, we are forced to question the origins of some of our assumptions about the novel as an art form. Whether our understanding of what constitutes a novel comes from a reading of Euro-American or African-American or African fiction will determine the kind of preconceptions we bring to her works.

How we approach the work of an African-American writer – the literary assumptions we bring to it and the critical methodologies we employ – has become an important issue in African-American literary criticism. Some of the African-American critics whose opinions we will encounter have been resistant to certain trends in Euro-American criticism while others have also rejected established methodologies and assumptions in African-American scholarship. The purpose of this introduction is to provide contexts for discussing Morrison's novels as African-American works. These contexts are discussed in the following order: Morrison's life; some of the key issues in African-American criticism; Morrison as a black woman writer; and the nature of the novel itself. In doing so we have identified some of those aspects of Euro-American literary scholarship to which a number of black critics have been resistant. The intention has also been to emphasise that Morrison's innovative novels are not simply reactions to or inversions of European models, but, because of their African-American origins, attempt to pursue subjects and narrative possibilities which had not been previously realised in fiction.

II

Black literary criticism has been resistant to the various trends, such as structuralism, in Euro-American critical practice which posit the separation of the literary text from its author, partly because reclaiming an identity and (narrative) voice to counter centuries of denial and misrepresentation is central to much post-colonial writing. However, a major reason for this reluctance to divorce text completely from its social and political context is that literature would lose its social function. For African and African-American writers the novel has been an important vehicle to represent the social context, to expose inequality, racism and social injustice.

From the point of view of European literary criticism, it is problematic to begin a study such as this with an account of the life of the author under consideration even though readers who are unfamiliar with an author's works often like to know something of the writer in order to get their bearings, whilst the enthusiasm of devotees invariably extends unashamedly to the life behind the books. Modern Euro-American criticism avoids speculative and mechanistic readings of works in the light of an author's biography together with problematic assumptions of authorial intention. The trend in Euopean criticism has

been to focus upon the act of reading itself and how the reader generates
meaning in a text. However, even if we accept European reservations
about acknowledging biographical contexts, it does not have to mean
that we must kill off the author as some European critics such as Barthes
have intimated. In the light of insights gleaned from modern European
criticism, we might retain an interest in a text's social and biographical
origins but be more properly cautious. In fleshing out the name on the
cover, we might be more aware of our own preconceptions; of how it is
our own reading which generates the meaning of a text; and of how works
do not have single or totally conscious or fixed points of origin.

The biographical context for Morrison's novels as African-American
works is approached, then, with these reservations in mind together
with an acknowledgement of the importance attached to the reclamation of an identity and a voice in black writing. Of course, all these
issues aside, Morrison's own life could be rendered from such a wide
range of multiple, overlapping and even possibly contradictory
perspectives that it would be futile in anything less than a biography, if
even there, to pretend to do it justice.

A biographical framework, which is all that remains possible in the
space which this short study permits, traditionally begins with the
place and date of an author's birth. Toni Morrison was born Chloe
Anthony Wofford, the second of four children, in Lorain, Ohio, in 1931.
Both her parents came from Southern families. Her maternal
grandparents, from Greenville and Birmingham, Alabama, had moved
to Lorain via Kentucky where her grandfather worked as a coal miner,
while her father had come to Ohio to escape the racial violence of
Georgia. As a State, Ohio embraced in microcosm the schizophrenic
nature of the Union itself in which the free states of the North and the
slave states of the South were brought together under one umbrella. As
Morrison recalls in an interview with Claudia Tate (1985):

> Ohio is an interesting and complex state. It has both a southern and
> a northern disposition. The Ohio River has historically represented
> freedom . . . The northern part of the state had underground railway
> stations and a history of black people escaping into Canada, but the
> southern part of the state is as much Kentucky as there is, complete
> with cross burnings. Ohio is a curious juxtaposition of what was
> ideal in this country and what was base. (119)

Notwithstanding the above notes of caution from European criticism, I
would argue that the way in which Morrison professes to see Ohio is

not irrelevant to her work. Perhaps in her own perspective on the State lie the origins of two of the major preoccupations of the novels: the pursuit of individual advancement by black people in a white-determined nation and culture at the expense of their black ancestry; and the reclamation of black solidarity based upon, to use her own word from *Beloved* (1987), 'rememory' of slavery and white America's continual denial of black people.

When Morrison lived there, Lorain was a steel mill town on Lake Erie with a population of approximately 30,000. Workers were drawn to its shipyards and steel mills in the 1920s and many of the migrant workers were blacks attracted there after they lost their lands as sharecroppers in the South. Sharecropping, where a cropper would work for a planter in return for a share of the crop at harvest time, had replaced the old slave plantations, but it was a precarious existence which locked the cropper in a cycle of dependency and despair, in contrast to which, the industry of the North seemed a bright prospect. For many of these people it was an especially cruel fate when the town was hit by the Depression and only in 1949 did Morrison's own father regain financial stability. Nevertheless Lorain provided black migrants from the South with a town where apparently class mattered more than race. Indeed Mbalia (1991), demonstrating the black critic's interest in the social context of literature, traces Morrison's own interest in class to her upbringing in Lorain.

Although there were no black ghettoes in Lorain, it was there, according to her own accounts, that Morrison had her first experiences of racism and it would be perverse to discuss the work of a black writer outside the context of these kinds of origins. One such experience, or more likely a combination of such experiences, undoubtedly gave rise to the episode early in *The Bluest Eye* (1970) involving Pecola and a white immigrant shopkeeper:

> She does not know what keeps his glance suspended. Perhaps because he is grown, or a man, and she a little girl. But she has seen interest, disgust, even anger in grown male eyes. Yet this vacuum is not new to her. It has an edge; somewhere in the bottom lid is the distaste. (36)

But Morrison's work does not only focus on black experience of white racism. There is a recurring interest in black people who have acquired social status through accommodating themselves to white society and by appropriating white values. Of course Morrison herself has been very successful as a writer and as a university teacher. Apart from winning the Nobel Prize for Literature (1993), she won the 1988 Pulitzer Prize for fiction for *Beloved* (1987) and the 1978 National Critics' Circle Award for fiction and the American Academy and Institute of Arts and Letters Award for *Song of Solomon* (1977). The novel proved a paperback bestseller with 570,000 copies in print. After the publication of *Tar Baby* (1981), which remained on the *New York Times'* bestseller list for four months, she became the first African-American woman to appear on the cover of *Newsweek*. She has achieved professorial status with the Schweitzer Chair at the State University of New York, Albany, and latterly, the Robert F. Goheen Chair, Council of the Humanities, Princeton University. But, unlike some of her characters, she cannot be accused of emulating white cultural values because she was educated at America's most distinguished black university, Howard University, Washington. In 1949 Washington was deeply caste-conscious and Morrison recalls in an interview with Nadelson in *The Guardian* in 1987:

> Thinking on it now I suppose I was backward, but I never longed for social integration with white people. For a place to pee when shopping, yes, but I was prey to the racism of my early years in Lorain where the only truly interesting people to me were the black people.

Here Morrison may be revealing the influence of her father who believed that, as Mbalia (1991) points out, all African people were superior to Europeans because as the victims of white racism they occupied a morally superior position in society (102). Like Guitar in *Song of Solomon* (1977) and Son in *Tar Baby* (1981), he believed that harmony could never exist between the races. Her father's views are voiced by Son in *Tar Baby* when he tells Jadine that black people and white people should work together but not sleep or even eat together.

While Son's viewpoint is one that is explored and debated in a number of the novels, the way in which Morrison writes from a black centre and the way in which white people are at the margins of her work, if they occur at all, is a subject to which she has returned in a number of interviews. For example, in Tate (1985) she explains:

> When I view the world, perceive it and write about it, it's the world of black people. It's not that I won't write about white people. I just

know that when I'm trying to develop the various themes I write about, the people who best manifest those themes for me are the black people whom I invent. It's not deliberate or calculated or self-consciously black, because I recognize and despise the artificial black writing some writers do. I feel them slumming among black people. (118)

The majority of the courses which Morrison followed at Howard University did not explore black history or culture. In an interview with Christopher Bigsby (1992), she recalls how her suggestion to write a term paper on black characters in Shakespeare was treated with derision. The apathy which such courses created among a large number of the university's students has been recalled by Mbalia (1991, 105–6) and is recreated in Milkman's attitudes in *Song of Solomon* (1977) that so exasperate Guitar. In the early 1960s, until his note to Hagar which breaks off their fourteen-year relationship, Milkman's life is one good time after another. In his own words, he is going 'wherever the party is' and is oblivious, as Melissa Walker (1991) points out, of the Montgomery bus boycott, the violent confrontations over integrated schooling in the South, the sit-ins and freedom rides. In the wake of the Supreme Court order of 1954, the late 1950s and the 1960s saw a rising tide of anti-discrimination boycotts and outbursts of ghetto violence, evidence of a new spirit of anger and defiance, which culminated in the Black Power movement, determined to bring to an end for once and for all black dependency on white power structures.

After graduating from Howard University, where she changed her name to Toni, Morrison earned a Master's degree at Cornell University for a thesis on Faulkner and Virginia Woolf. This was followed by a period of teaching at Texas Southern University following which Morrison returned to Howard University in 1957 as a Faculty member. In the meantime, while a postgraduate student she had married a Jamaican architect by whom she had two sons, Harold and Slade. During her time as a teacher at Howard University she taught two of those who subsequently took a leading role in the emerging black civil rights movement: Stokely Carmichael, founder of the Black Power movement, and Claude Brown. In her interview with Bigsby (1992), she recalls how Brown asked her to help revise *Manchild in the Promised Land* for five cents a page! However, during her time at the university, she did not take an active role in the civil rights movement herself. One of the reasons for this was the birth of her son in 1961, but another was that she was not a fully committed integrationalist even though she recognised that segregation served the interests of the white racists. A further explanation may have been that, as Butler-Evans (1989) has pointed out, in the 1960s race rather than gender had become the overriding sign for the oppression of black people so that the political agenda was dominated by black men. Indeed the absence of a political presence and the suppression of an alternative voice impeded the emergence of a black feminist literature. Moreover, the emergent white liberal feminist movement of the 1960s and 1970s failed to address issues related to black women. Nevertheless, a number of the events which were taken up by the civil rights movement obviously affected Morrison deeply and were incorporated in her novels. *Song of Solomon* (1977), for example, makes specific reference to the brutal killing of Emmett Louis 'Bobo' Till, a 14 year old, who was flogged, mutilated, lynched, shot in the head, and thrown into the Tallahatchie River with a 70 pound cotton gin fan round his neck for allegedly whistling after a white woman. Secondly, the event which triggers Guitar's search for money is the bombing in church of four little African girls on 15 September 1963, in Birmingham, Alabama.

In the mid-1960s, with a dissolved relationship and two children to support, Morrison left teaching to work in the textbook subsidiary of Random House at Syracuse. Mbalia (1991) is the only scholar to have attached significance to this in terms of the development of her political consciousness. Yet while working here, Morrison edited *The West and the Rest of Us* by the leading African historian Chinweizu, two of the arguments of which are reflected in the novels that followed. *Song of Solomon* (1977) and *Tar Baby* (1981) both explore on some level how capitalism gives rise to and maintains racism and how, in keeping with Chinweizu's thesis, white power gives rise to white racism whilst white racism in turn serves white power. Moreover, Chinweizu's thesis that some African people have been so brainwashed by European propaganda that self-hatred characterises the African petty bourgeois must have encouraged Morrison to pursue her interest in what drove some African-Americans to seek a white American identity.

Morrison began work on her first novel, *The Bluest Eye* (1970), at the age of 30 while teaching at Howard University. It was a long process because she kept revising her ideas and because she was conscious of herself as a black woman entering a field where the high ground was held by whites. Not wanting her employer to know she was publishing with another Press, when the book was eventually published her new

identity emerged along with it because she changed her name and even
withheld her photograph from the book jacket. Given the recurring
concern in her work with the search for identity and with the
significance of names for black people, this is probably one of the most
interesting biographical details about her as far as the novels
themselves are concerned. It highlights her conviction that black
people, at the level of the personal self, have the capacity to 'invent
themselves' and, as we shall see, this is a significant trope in most of her
novels.

Much of her first novel was written in the evenings while her children
were in bed and we can see the influence of her position as a woman
bringing up two children alone. It was the first novel to give a black
child centre stage; previously, the black child had not only been
peripheral, but doubly marginalised as a comic figure. The negative
portrayal of black children and black people generally is a familiar
theme within white fiction which post-structuralist and post-colonial
literary criticism have increasingly identified. As a device by which one
cultural position has been legitimated over another, it is analogous to
the portrayal of the Welsh and Irish in English fiction and popular
culture.

Unlike Maya Angelou, Morrison puts very little of her own life into
her writings. However, much of what she read appears to have
provided important source material. While Senior Editor at Random
House, Morrison brought several black writers, for example, Angela
Davies, Toni Cade Bambara and Gayl Jones, to the publication list.
The influence of Henry Dumas, whose work she read in the early 1970s
and for whom she helped to organise a book party in October 1974, has
been identified as particularly important. Mbalia (1991) for example
points out that his work incorporates surrealism, supernaturalism,
magic, astrology, myth and science fiction, all elements to be found in a
concentrated form in Morrison's *Song of Solomon* (1977). Certainly
Morrison borrowed the name of Dumas's racist Arkansas home town,
Sweet Home, for the plantation in *Beloved* (1987) where she also uses
the Dumas name Heyboy (Mbalia, 1991, 112).

Song of Solomon (1977) which went on to win the 1978 National Book
Critics' Circle Award, proved a turning point for Morrison because it
was then that she began to think of herself as a writer rather than an
editor who wrote, but her international reputation was established
when *Beloved* (1987) won the Pulitzer Prize. Between *Song of Solomon* and
Beloved (1987), apart from *Tar Baby* (1981), Morrison published her

first play, based on the brutal murder of Emmett Till which she had previously incorporated into *Song of Solomon. Dreaming Emmett* was produced by the Capital Repertory Company in 1986. As Wilkerson (1988) explains, the play, which uses a dream metaphor, is concerned with the meanings attached to this lynching, 'at once a poignant metaphor for the history of black–white relationships and a profoundly disturbing historical moment in the national consciousness' (185). Several features of the play emphasise the importance of the community in black culture. For example, the influence of the African dilemma tale – a traditional oral narrative which puts a dilemma to the community for it to resolve – is evident in the dialectic which the play establishes with its audience. They are encouraged to enter into a debate with what is happening on stage when a woman of the 1980s emerges from among them to challenge Emmett who until this point in the play was dreaming only of revenge on his killers. Moreover, the way in which those on trial appear in elaborate masks which they strip off to reveal further layers of masks recalls African masked drama, one of the functions of which, as Segy (1976) argues, was rooted in a communal need to participate in a collective consciousness. In its concern with community, the play develops and merges two positions which are explored further in *Beloved*: that individuals and their family histories are embedded in their people's history and that the emancipation of black people can only be realised within the contexts of black communities and black culture.

Beloved is based upon the true story of an escaped slave, Margaret Garner, who tried to kill herself and her children rather than return to slavery. She was not tried for murder, which was hardly considered a crime for a black woman, but for stealing, in effect, her master's property – herself! Although the story was well known, Morrison may have drawn on *The Black Book*, a compendium of newscuttings and advertisements chronicling the life of African people in the United States from slavery to the civil rights movement. In her interview with Christopher Bigsby, Morrison reveals that her original project was a single work, entitled *Beloved*, which was to have centred on three events separated from one another by 50 or 60 years. However, the publisher chose to issue the first part as a novel in its own right, leaving the other two parts to form two further novels.

The award of the Nobel Prize to Morrison in October 1993 attracted a certain amount of controversy. Other black writers have won the Nobel Prize – Wole Soyinka, the playwright from Nigeria, and Derek

Walcott, the poet from the West Indies – but Toni Morrison is the first African-American to do so. Within this context, the award might be seen as the acknowledgement of a writer from a body of literature which had been neglected for too long. However, at the time the award did not meet with universal approval among black writers and intellectuals. Toni Morrison was seen as representative of a small coterie of black women writers such as Maya Angelou, Alice Walker and Gloria Naylor favoured by the white literary and academic establishment. Other black writers such as Charles Johnson and Stanley Crouch alleged that it was a triumph of 'political correctness', an endorsement of a writer from a marginalised culture who suited the taste of the dominant culture. No doubt politics play a part in the award of the Nobel Prize, but such speculation is not the concern here. In the media's coverage of Morrison's award, dissent was newsworthy and controversy worth encouraging for the sake of readership as well as debate. The dissent often focused on criticisms which seriously misrepresented Morrison's work. It was argued that she betrayed her origins as a black writer by employing European models. She was not judged a good novelist because her characters were said to have no social context; they were found to be stereotypes, thinly drawn to convey messages that could not be easily understood. Her work was even said not to challenge stereotypes of black people. Such attacks on Morrison's work betrayed a profound failure to appreciate how her writing has challenged conventional perceptions not only of black culture and black people, but of the nature and potential of the novel itself. It also demonstrates an appalling ignorance on the part of some leading writers and academics of the scholarship, much of it by African-American academics, on her work.

In addition to the novels, Morrison has produced an important critical work, *Playing in the Dark: Whiteness and the Literary Imagination* (1992) which arose out of the way in which her fiction required her 'to think about how free I can be as an African-American woman writer in my genderized, sexualized, wholly racialized world' (4). The study turns white criticism of American literature on its head; instead of seeing African-Americans as on the margins of the literary canon, the American literary tradition is seen as centred upon them:

> These speculations have led me to wonder whether the major and
> championed characteristics of our national literature – individualism,
> masculinity, social engagement versus historical isolation; acute and

ambiguous moral problematics; the thematics of innocence coupled with an obsession with figurations of death and hell – are not in fact responses to a dark, abiding, signing Africanist presence. (5)

Morrison has also edited *Race-ing Justice, En-Gendering Power: Essays on Anita Hill, Clarence Thomas, and the Construction of Social Reality* (1993), a discussion of the ramifications of the United States Senate hearings in 1991 on the controversial, if not scandalous, nomination of Clarence Thomas to the Supreme Court, and the accusations of sexual harassment brought by Anita Hill. The essays constitute an important critical document on race, gender, politics and power structures in America as they have developed during Morrison's career as a writer.

III

Even a brief account of the biographical context of Morrison's novels is enough to alert us to the dangers of seeing them as purely reactive; for example, as inverting European ways of thinking, as reacting to white racism or subverting Euro-American aesthetic assumptions. This is a point worth pursuing in preparation for the discussion of the novels themselves. Firstly in relation to one critical approach to African-American writing which Morrison herself has felt strongly enough about to publicly reject. Secondly in the context of Morrison as a black woman and thirdly in relation to the Euro-American novel.

The extent to which African-American writing has been marginalised within the paradigms of Euro-American literary criticism has formed the centre of debate among a number of African-American critics. This debate about the relationship of black writing to Euro-American critical practice has focused on whether it should be approached as a separatist or syncretist literature. At one extreme there has been a tendency to adopt a separatist model of African-American literature, to see it located within a tradition that is African rather than American. The major advantage of this approach has been to lift African-American literature out of its marginalised position within Euro-American critical traditions. Critics working with this model have been able to highlight the salient characteristics of African-American literature, for example the way in which it often draws on folklore and myth as indices of an alternative ontology, which generally have not been given sufficient attention by critics using the norms of Euro-

American literature as a touchstone for evaluation. However the weakness of this model is that it ignores the syncretist nature of many African-American texts. In other words, African-American writers are often the products of hybrid cultural experiences and frequently draw from both African and European heritages. As de Weever (1991) emphasises, 'the Black-American branch produces a literature in which African and African-American traditions are blended. Neither completely African nor completely Euro-American, this new blend is just as firmly American as the novels previously defined as American because this flower can bloom nowhere else' (22).

The difficulty of achieving a properly balanced critical approach to African-American writing is exemplified in the application of the 'magic realist' model which has been suggested by Slemon (1989) as appropriate to post-colonial texts. The term was first coined by Franz Roh in 1925 in relation to post-expressionist art and since the 1940s it has been slapped wholesale on to novels by Latin American writers to emphasise their difference from mainstream culture. The term is now applied to writers from outside Latin America, including, for example, those from the Caribbean, Nigeria and India.

One of the difficulties in applying this concept to such a wide range of literatures is that it has not been rigorously defined or adequately distinguished from related literary concepts such as fabulation, the fantastic and the uncanny. However, Isabel Allende's definition (Lewis, 1993) of 'magic realism' suggests many of the features and concerns of Morrison's novels:

> Magic realism really means allowing a place in literature to the invisible forces that have such a powerful place in life . . . dreams, myth, legend, passion, obsession, superstition, religion, the overwhelming power of nature and the supernatural. All these are present in African poetry, Hindu sagas, Arab tales, and used to be present in Western literature up to the Gothic novel and Edgar Allen Poe. Only in the past few decades have they been excluded by white male authors who decided that whatever cannot be controlled doesn't exist. (26)

Indeed the application of the term 'magic realism' to post-colonial literature generally has helped critics to highlight some of its distinguishing characteristics. Slemon (1989), drawing on the work of Kroetsch and of Kenyon, argues that the label is especially appropriate to texts written on the margins, as it were, and 'can itself signify resistance to central assimilation by more stable generic systems' (10). In 'magic realism', as Allende's definition suggests, the representational code of realism is locked in a continuous dialectic with that of fantasy. As we shall see in the course of this study, such a dialectic permeates Morrison's texts. But Slemon identifies a further feature which is even more relevant to Morrison's work because it highlights two opposing systems of language: 'a dialectic between "codes of recognition" inherent within the inherited language and those imagined codes – perhaps utopian or future-orientated – that characterize a culture's "original relations" with the world' (11).

Morrison's novels frequently return the reader, directly or indirectly, to how inherited Euro-American language organises and structures its culture's relations with the world so as to exclude Africa-Americans or at best to marginalise them. Indeed this is the explicit subject of her first novel, the strengths of which have still not been fully appreciated by critics. But the weakness of 'magic realism' as a point of entry into Morrison's work, even when it is fully defined, as by Allende, is that it can overemphasise a non-black cultural legacy and lead us to underestimate the cultural paradigms in which she works as an African-American author. In fact in an interview with Paul Gilroy (1993), Morrison rejects the label because it denies the cultural origins of her writings: 'Just as long as they don't call me a magic realist, as though I don't have a culture to write out of. As though that culture has no intellect' (181).

IV

Although the 'magic realist' model highlights a number of key features of Morrison's novels, then, it can lead to an overemphasis upon them as reactions to non-African-American literary conventions. As we said at the outset, it is such an overemphasis which this study of Morrison's work has sought to counter. The focus falls, therefore, on how each of the novels pursues what has not been previously articulated. The desirability of such an approach, avoiding overstressing the subversive or reactive nature of Morrison's work, is especially apparent in our second area of focus, Toni Morrison as a black woman writer. Despite being sometimes contradictory on the subject in interview, Morrison writes as a black woman with the experiences of black women in mind.

On radio in 1983, while claiming at first to write 'without gender focus', Morrison, backtracking quickly, affirmed: 'I am valuable as a writer because I am a woman, because women, it seems to me, have some special knowledge about certain things'. She has advanced this position less diffidently in subsequent interviews including, for example, that with Sandi Russell (1986): 'I write for black women. We are not addressing the men, as some white female writers do. We are not attacking each other, as both black and white men do. Black women writers look at things in an unforgiving/loving way. They are writing to repossess, re-name, re-own' (Mackay, 1988, 54 and 46). Indeed the experiences of repossessing and reclaiming are crucial for black women writers who start from an especially difficult position which has been summarised by Susheila Nasta (1991):

> Whilst, for instance, there are obvious parallels between the experience of women's oppression in previously colonised territories and women's oppression worldwide, there is a danger even in western feminist literary circles (which often have failed to give full critical attention to literary works by black women writers) of being seduced by easy notions of a 'universal feminism'. The post-colonial woman writer is not only involved in making herself heard, in changing the architecture of male-centred ideologies and languages, or in discovering new forms and language to express her experience, she has also to subvert and demythologise indigenous male writings and traditions which seek to label her. (xv)

This difficult position has caused some African-American critics to emphasise how Morrison's novels invert familiar myths and stereo-types of black women. For example, de Weever (1991) argues that Morrison evokes a range of mythical mother figures, such as that of the nurturing mother who devours her children, as a reaction to the stereotype of the black mother (134). The black Mammy is the legendary figure of sentimental novels and popular films; obedient, obliging, cheerful, resilient and resourceful. It is an especially damaging stereotype because it legitimises motherhood as the female function most commonly associated with black women. As such the black mother provides a powerful example of how inherited Euro-American language organises and shapes our perceptions of black people and we can understand how any black writer needs to subvert this stereotype. Yet whilst African-American writers must be aware of these stereotypes and how they impinge upon their narratives, they usually write out of a fully-realised sense of the actual lived experiences of black people which involves more than responding to Euro-American stereotypes. The Euro-American stereotype, even allowing for the fact that the circumstances and conditions of their lives have forced black women to function chiefly as mothers, as de Weever (1991) argues (134), ignores many dimensions and strengths of black women. These qualities, rather than simply a desire to subvert stereotypes, drive Morrison's characterisations of black women.

On one level de Weever's (1991) characterisation of Eva in *Sula* as a figure of death is insightful, providing a fuller mythical context for the character. The facts that she has lost a leg in an accident and has such projections of sleeping with her son that she sets him on fire, do link her to those mythical figures who have committed incest and who are either lame or walk with difficulty (108). Indeed it is sometimes the mythical element of, for example, Eva in *Sula* and Pilate in *Song of Solomon*, who, like Eve, has no navel, which separates these women from the stereotypes of the black mother. But we must not lose sight of the fact that Eva is created out of the lived experiences of black women. Eva's sacrifice of her leg, after all, is an index of her courage, her commitment to her children and her independence of mind – strengths which the Euro-American stereotype denies. It is not surprising that black women writers often do not provide romantic, conventional portrayals of motherhood and that instead of the Mammy figure they portray heroines who seek psychic development on their own terms. de Weever points out what she should not have to point out to many women, let alone many African-American women, that 'motherhood is thus not an ideal condition' (157). Her emphasis falls upon how 'the cultural myth of the black mammy, that all-nurturing, all-patient, all-loving, all-accepting woman, is invented to show that she does not exist in reality' (ibid.).

The work of many African-American writers, and especially the novels of Toni Morrison, then, do not simply invert Euro-American stereotypes. They give expression to desires, needs and aspirations which are not articulated by cultural myths such as that of the black mother. Throughout Morrison's work, there is a recurring concern with black, female-headed households where survival, as the German scholar Koenen (1985) points out, is dependent upon 'self-inventing' (McKay, 1988, 199). Although this process of 'self-inventing' does not always bring success on a personal or social level, Koenen's theory of

'generational degeneration' in Morrison's novels – the farther down the
generations of women the weaker their personalities become – is
simplistic. It ignores how although the personalities of the daughters
are weaker than their mothers – Hannah is weaker than Eva and Reba
is weaker than Pilate – the personalities of the grand-daughters are
usually very strong. Indeed their level of 'self-inventing', as we shall
discuss later in the chapter on *Sula*, is disturbing because it is so self-
obsessed. Morrison's novels argue that black people's emancipation
can only be realised within the context of black culture and the black
community. Although this always works so as to criticise aspects of the
strong grand-daughters, Morrison's novels are usually even more
critical of women, like Nel in *Sula*, who are role-bound and unable to
break out of their oppression.

V

The ways in which Morrison's texts allow a place in literature to 'myth,
legend, passion, obsession, superstition, religion, the overwhelming
power of nature and the supernatural', then, are not attempts to invert
Euro-American literary conventions. The application of Gérard
Genette's model of narrative to Morrison's work highlights how it
extends the creative possibilities of narrative without us having to see
Morrison's work as a response to the Euro-American novel. Genette's
model presupposes that a narrative, like a sentence, can be divided for
study into its component parts. Narratives do not only function at the
level of characters, events and places; they operate at the level of their
narration, the way the narrative is constructed. In considering the work
of Toni Morrison, it is impossible not to be aware of how the succession
of events – identified by Genette in 1972 as the 'histoire' (the 'story') –
is broken up in the telling – what Genette called the 'récit' (the
'narrative') – and rearranged so that often characters are not even
presented in relation to each other in ways that make immediate or
complete sense. In *Beloved*, especially, the action is not presented
chronologically but in a dislocated temporal scheme.

In our reading, we tend to be conditioned by the conventions of
traditional first or third person narratives, expecting coherence and
consistency, and presuming that the narrator's perspective is synonymous with that of the figure in the text through whose eyes the
events are seen. Genette's identification of the actual telling or

'narrating' of the story as an area of study in addition to the ways in which the story is constructed – 'récit' – provides a means of appreciating the innovative nature of Morrison's novels. The narrative itself often moves backwards and forwards in time, shifting perspectives and plunging into internal longings. At times it takes external leaps and even hands over the narrating, as in *The Bluest Eye*, *Beloved* and *Jazz*, to other voices so that it is important in Morrison's work to distinguish between what Genette calls the 'focalizer' and the narrator. In classic realist novels there is often no distinction between the narrator and the character which focuses the narrator's point of view. The unification of the focaliser and the narrator, as is the case with many nineteenth-century European texts, produces a more unified and coherent worldview than when the two are divided, as in many of Morrison's novels. The use of different narrators and the exploration of the creative potential of separating narrator and focaliser in Morrison's work should be seen as being proactive in an African-American context rather than being reactive to a European tradition. Often the different narrators are a means of exploring how discourses which operate in society around subjects such as gender and race are unquestioned and are taken for truth. As we shall see in the discussion of the novels themselves, the space that opens between the narrator(s) and the focaliser(s) challenges the imposition of singular unified perspectives and promotes a plurality of worldviews.

The dénouements of many of Morrison's novels favour community, the moral responsibility of individuals to each other, the reclamation of traditional black values and the importance of the ancestor. But as a writer she appears, from the evidence of her texts, to be drawn – almost paradoxically – toward the dramatic potential of enigma, distances, spaces, dislocation, alienation, gaps and ellipses. Although this may be because few writers can resist these sources of drama, it may also be the product of the particular milieu in which Morrison began to write. In the late 1960s and early 1970s, distances, divisions and debates opened up for the first time in African-American writing around the subject of black identity. Two novels published in 1970 in particular – Toni Morrison's *The Bluest Eye* and Alice Walker's *The Third Life of Grange Copeland* – shifted the focus of African-American fiction. The different addresses of these novels, despite or rather because of their acknowledgement of conflict and division, reflect the enhanced confidence in black experience as literary material and a wider reassessment of monolithic and monologic versions of black identity. Black fiction in the 1970s and 1980s moved away from a homogenised sense of a unified and unifying black community and from overreliance upon the binarism of positive/negative images of black people. It tended instead to engage with a pluralistic sense of experience, incorporating the multiple subjectivities which constitute any individual's sense of identity. Issues of ethnicity were explored within a larger hierarchy of articulated differences: racial, gendered, cultural and sexual.

Toni Morrison's summary in LeClair (1981) of what she is trying to achieve in her fiction encapsulates the complexity of many black novels written during this period:

> I am not explaining anything to anybody. My work bears witness and suggests who the outlaws were, who survived under what circumstances and why, what was legal in the community as opposed to what was legal outside it. All that is in the fabric of the story in order to do what the music used to do. (26)

For Morrison, the development of black fiction became important because of the loss of black oral traditions and the appropriation of black music by the dominant culture. The novel provides the possibility of 'becom(ing) coherent in the world':

> There has to be a mode to do what music did for blacks, what we used to be able to do in private and in that civilization that existed underneath the white civilization. (26)

Of course, as we suggested above, this does not mean that Morrison's novels themselves are necessarily as coherent as narratives as are many European novels. In fact they tend towards what the Russian critic, Bakhtin (1975), characterised as 'dialogical', where there is constant interaction between meanings, all of which have the potential for conditioning others (411ff). Morrison, like Dostoevsky whom Bakhtin identified as an example of a dialogical novelist, is always sensitive to, indeed her fiction is founded upon, the existence of multi-layered and competing discourses. As we shall see, concepts such as community, authority, individuality and moral responsibility are subject to scrutiny in Morrison's work. Her texts appear to reject, as one would expect of works written by a black writer, the confidence of the Western philosophical tradition in its modes of ordering and classification. Generally speaking, no one character in a Morrison novel is responsible for giving us the whole truth, if ever such exists. The oppositional narrative modes which we identified earlier – realism and fantasy – are, like the voices in a dialogical novel, in continuous struggle to become the language of truth.

As we shall discuss in more detail in the course of this book, there are strong elements of fantasy, recurring non-realistic structures, in Morrison's novels: for example, Pecola's obsession with blue eyes; Sula watching her own mother burn to death; Pilate's absence of a navel; Ruth's obsessive breastfeeding of her son and necrophilic love for her father; the myth of Solomon's leap; the presence of house number 126; the appearance and dismemberment of Beloved; the concept of rememory. Whilst critics such as de Weever (1991) have drawn attention to the openness of African-American narratives, of which Morrison's use of fantasy is an example, this feature has not been placed in a wider theoretical context. In fact Bakhtin's identification of the inconclusiveness of the novel as a genre in 'Epic and Novel', that it is always in process of development, can help us to understand how, in the hands of black writers, it has proved such a popular vehicle for non-European subjects and worldviews and has been able to incorporate, as we shall see, the openness of traditional black culture. The way in which the novel, as Bakhtin argues, incorporates other genres in its own peculiar structure, reformulating and reaccentuating them, helps explain how African-American fiction has given a frame and coherence to materials drawn from African, American and European cultural traditions as well as from indigenous oral traditions and folklore.

Although Bakhtin is a European critic, he provides a model of the novel which is appropriate to work by African-American writers. Generally the parameters of Anglo-American criticism often preclude discussion of how African-American writers have extended the creative possibilities of the genre and have created space for concerns, preoccupations and devices more common in African and Latin American than European literature. Anglo-American criticism, for example, has tended to follow Henry James's disapproval of untidiness in narrative and has paid insufficient regard to the fact that loose ends can serve profound aesthetic and philosophical purposes (Gibson, 1990, 170–1). As de Weever (1991) reveals, the open endedness of Morrison's novels seems inevitable as the author resists firm closure (40). Instead her works often end with moments of insight: at the end of *Sula* (1973), as de Weever says, Nel realises that she has been lonely for Sula and not for Jude; at the end of *The Bluest Eye* (1970), Claudia realises that the townspeople have made Pecola their scapegoat. Or as with *Song of Solomon* (1977) and *Tar Baby* (1981), they are inconclusive and leave many questions unresolved. Indeed in order to appreciate the creative possibilities of the novel as an art form, and to understand how Morrison's work extends the dimensions of narrative, we have to place a greater value than previously on incompleteness, disruption, confusion, contradiction, internal inconsistencies and unfulfilled expectations.

Many African-American novels deliberately subvert traditional white expectations in their sense of structure and their use of language. But it would be limiting to consider African-American fiction only against a backdrop of the Euro-American novel. It is important to bear in mind that the emphasis on closure which we find in much white fiction has left the full potential of narrative undeveloped. It should not surprise us to find that fiction in other cultures has taken advantage of possibilities which an Anglo-American/European aestheticism has tended to discourage. An insightful and profitable approach to the open endedness of Morrison's work is to think of it as a response to the potential and open endedness of narrative *per se*.

VI

In summary, it is often the application of principles and methodologies established in European literary criticism to African-American writing that creates the major problems and raises the key issues. Concepts such as linearity, progress and chronology are not appropriate to the works of many African-American writers and certainly not to Morrison's novels which are evolutionary, circular, repetitive, contradictory and ambiguous, with characters whose histories are generally revealed in fragments from a variety of sources. There is a canon of literary criticism just as there is a canon of literary texts. Ironically, contemporary literary criticism has exposed the Euro-American literary canon as an ideological construction favouring white, male viewpoints. But the way in which literary criticism sustains, protects and privileges Euro-American perspectives has not been subject to the same scrutiny. African-American scholars have become increasingly sceptical of this critical and theoretical hegemony. This introduction has sought to recommend an approach which recognises the innovative form and content of the novels themselves without seeing them as reactions to European models. Such an emphasis upon the novel as a literary text according to some critics is new to African-American criticism. For as de Weever (1991) argues, until the social movements of the 1960s, our definitions of American literature were determined by the Attic-Hebraic-Christian traditions that make up European culture (21). Morrison herself has complained in Tate (1985) that the work of African-Americans has tended to be approached from a sociological perspective, as resource rather than text:

> Critics generally don't associate black people with ideas. They see marginal people; they just see another story about black folks. They regard the whole thing as sociologically interesting perhaps but very parochial. There's a notion out there in the land that there are human beings one writes about, and then there are black people or Indians or some other marginal group. (121)

Her complaint has been echoed by a leading critic of black literature, Henry Louis Gates, Jr (1984):

> If Euro-Americans have used the creative writing of Afro-Americans primarily as evidence of the blacks' mental or social 'perfectibility' or as a measure of the blacks' 'racial' psychology or sociology, then they have used African literature as evidence of African 'anthropology', of traditional and modern African customs and beliefs. (5)

Gates, Jr, believes that 'because of this curious valorization of the social and polemical functions of black literature, the structure of the black text has been *repressed* and treated as if it were *transparent*'.

This study of Morrison's novels focuses upon their language and how they are constructed; upon various methods of unlocking their multiple meanings; and upon how other texts impose meanings upon them. It employs a number of perspectives on language, meaning, narrative and history which are normally placed under the general label of post-structuralist. Although these theories are not as homogeneous as that label might suggest, they do coincide around challenges to the nature of language and to the concept of the individual. Post-structuralist theories of language draw attention to the need for us to question the relationship between language, meaning and what we normally regard as 'social reality' more than we usually do. Language does not merely reflect 'reality', it constructs it. The language which we use to construct what we think is 'reality' contains preconceptions and assumptions which are imposed, sometimes unconsciously, on what we are describing. Language is not a transparent window on to the world; it is more like a stained glass window which distorts and colours what we see through it. As we shall discover, the fact that language can never be ideologically innocent or neutral is one of the subjects of many of Morrison's novels. But they are also concerned with the way in which language enables certain discourses to circulate and achieve priority over others. These discourses which circulate around, for example, gender and race, and which are often institutionalised in, for example, the family, education and the legal system, pass for truth whilst privileging certain groups such as white, Anglo-Saxon males and denying the legitimacy of others such as the black working class. Post-structuralist theories of discourse and history challenge the way we have tended to think of the individual in literary criticism in liberal humanist terms as a free-thinking, autonomous being by suggesting that we are all the products of discourses which are historically specific. This takes us to the core of much black writing where, although the free-thinking being may still be an ideal, the individual is inevitably perceived as the subject of a political state, susceptible to the forces of control which operate in a given society or social context, and constructed through language or discourse.

As we said at the outset, the study of the novels which follows has sought to respect both their specificity and the ways in which they relate to each other. Discussions of individual works are structured to help readers who may not be familiar with all Morrison's novels and they are designed to illuminate important interpretative issues in her work as a whole whilst providing extended treatment of topics and features particular to each book. The focus throughout is on the way in which Morrison's innovative form is driven by its radical content. In the discussion of *The Bluest Eye* the emphasis falls on the way language is enmeshed with power structures and the dominant social forms determining 'social reality'. It argues that the success of *The Bluest Eye* lies in the approaches and perspectives it brings to an exploration of the impact of prevailing white ideologies on the black community. In the next chapter, it is suggested that *Sula* too is not usefully approached through reading habits developed in relation to the realist European novel. A salient feature of the novel is the way in which it constantly requires readers to question their own reading of it. The focus, however, is on Sula herself in whom the African-American woman's need to create her own notion of selfhood is complicated by the characteristics she shares with the traditional figure of the African trickster. Chapter 4, on *Song of Solomon*, argues that this work especially may be too easily read as an ironic version of the European romance formula but that such an approach would overlook the importance of black concerns, African myth and African perspectives in the novel. The discussion of *Tar Baby* in chapter 5 develops many of the points raised in the chapters on *Sula* and *Song of Solomon* or approaches them from a different context. Whilst the novel's debt to African-American myth is apparent from its title, the chapter demonstrates some of the dangers in interpreting this too simply or too rigidly. Throughout, the focus is upon the complex process by which black people, especially black women, have to negotiate the competing discourses which influence individual and social behaviour. The way in which any novel consists of a transposition of material from different sources, both literary and non-literary, is the basis of the approach to *Beloved* in chapter 6. One of the most difficult of Morrison's novels because of its subject matter and fragmentary structure, it is also one of the most evocative, moving and cathartic. The chapter demonstrates how a preoccupation with unearthing narratives which have been hidden by or buried within other narratives is integral to the novel and explores the various levels of occlusion within it. In chapter 7 the final novel, *Jazz*, is recognised as significantly influenced by African-American music, but its experiments with form are seen as determined, like that of the other novels, by aspects of African-American history and experience which had not previously been articulated. The book concludes with a brief overview of the language in Morrison's novels and a postscript which attempts to take stock of her achievement to date whilst recognising hopefully that many works have yet to come.

2

The Bluest Eye (1970)

The innovatory nature of Morrison's first two novels is derived from the ways in which their radical content is allowed to determine their experiment with form. Ostensibly *The Bluest Eye* is about a lonely, victimised, black girl, Pecola Breedlove, who is driven insane by her desire to have white skin, blonde hair and blue eyes, and the interplay between her disintegration and a number of black characters who are more fully integrated into white society. But even a casual reader cannot help but notice that there is more to the book than this. At the outset of the novel Morrison adapts the eighteenth and nineteenth-century convention whereby work by a black American often carried a preface from a white writer confirming the authenticity of the black authorship. In its preface, which provides an introduction to some of the chapters, extracts from a Dick–Jane American primer present a standardised, white American family embracing Euro-American views of beauty and happiness. This introduces the major theme of *The Bluest Eye*, that the white voice is inappropriate to dictate the contours of African-American life. At the end of the novel Claudia and Frieda overhear snippets of gossip about the Breedloves that summarise the social consequences of this imposition: none of them seem 'right'; they don't have relatives; they are ugly. Beauty is as much a political as an aesthetic concept whilst ugliness is not merely a matter of appearance; it is a manifestation in Western thinking of an inner ugliness, a spiritual and moral failure, if not an innate evil:

> That which was 'white' (or Anglo, male, Christian, wealthy) was extolled and infused with connotations of benevolence and superi-

ority, while that which was not white (or not Anglo, female, non-Christian, poor) was debased and associated with malevolence and inferiority. (Braxton and McLaughlin, 1990, 153)

Claudia herself, as the mature narrator, condemns the American concept of blonde beauty as one of 'the most destructive ideas in the history of human thought' (95). As de Weever (1991) points out, the insistence upon one standard of beauty contradicts the pluralistic nature of contemporary America where African standards of beauty are frequently adopted by African-Americans, for example, the dashiki, ancient Egyptian long braids and cornrow hairstyles (107). She also surmises that there may have been secret societies in some African countries in the seventeenth and eighteenth centuries concerned to inculcate a confident centre of being in young girls and young women which was then destroyed by slavery and racism.

This chapter examines how the novel's structure is driven by its exploration of the impact of white ideologies on the black community. In particular it focuses on the ironic juxtaposition of the white mythology of the Dick–Jane primer and the lives of African-Americans as part of a larger interplay of differences within the novel and on how the exploration of the nature of whiteness provides its arguments about the embourgeoisement of black culture with a special slant. The order and the apparent moral certainty of the white world is contrasted with the inner dislocation and search for coherence in the lives of Pecola and her parents. The novel itself is organised into four sequences, each associated with a season and beginning with Claudia's memories of that season. There are seven subsections, introduced by lines taken from the primer extract in the preface, related from the perspective of an omniscient narrator. The lines, reprinted with punctuation and spaces removed, are ostensibly unintelligible so as to emphasise the dislocation between the white Dick–Jane mythology and the norms of black experience. The retrospective nature of Claudia's narrative is an important device in deconstructing the embourgeoisement of black people in the novel. At the end of the book we realise that the voice of Claudia, which becomes fused with that of the omniscient narrator, is that of an older Claudia who, now living in the North, is looking back and tracing the stages which have led to her maturity of outlook. Thus, on one level, the narrative takes us backwards from the present in the North into the past and the South, whilst, on another level, taking us forward in the events of Pecola's tragedy.

II

The text pursues ironies created by the interplay between two levels of articulation in the narrative. One level of articulation arises from the role of Claudia as survivor and her retrospective account of episodes introduced within the context of a season; the other derives from the black kinswoman who narrates the episodes introduced by extracts from the primer. She is an omniscient narrator who is able to provide access to information which Claudia could not have and is able to involve characters outside of Claudia's immediate range of experience. The ironies arising from these two levels of narration are developed within a wider framework provided by the mismatch between what the primer suggests is the norm and the lived experience of the black families.

In discussing the levels of irony within *The Bluest Eye* it is important to remember that Toni Morrison's works are not easily approached through reading habits developed in relation to the realist novel where language often gives the impression of transparency, that is where the representation and the represented are seen as the same thing. In Morrison's novels, language, as the French critic Roland Barthes recognised, is enmeshed with the power structures and forces underlying what we might call 'social reality': 'And the reason why power is invincible is that the object in which it is carried for all human eternity is language: the language that we speak and write' (Barthes, 1981, 459). In Morrison's novels, ideology is not, as envisaged by Marx, an illusion or false consciousness, but, as conceived by the French Marxist theorist, Louis Althusser, it is the staple of daily living, embodied in language and in social institutions such as the school, the family and the media.

As we said in the introduction, the dialectic between inherited codes of representation and imagined codes is one of the features which Morrison's work shares with novels from Latin America classified as 'magic realist'. This dialectic emerges in *The Bluest Eye*, as in subsequent novels, from the realisation of the black culture out of which Morrison is writing and of the distortion of self created by the imposition of white norms on black people. The effect of this imposition is to create a profound sense of fracture. The concept of black in the novel is a construct partly of the characters' own making but mostly social, based on white definitions of blackness which associate it with violence, poverty, dirt and lack of education, whilst Africa is perceived as uncivilised and (negatively) tribal. Black people developed as a social category of low status when Arab trade in African slaves increased, but it was with the European subordination of world peoples as labouring classes that blacks came to form, as McLaughlin says, part of an oppositional and hierarchical system of cultural constructs that justified a coloniser/colonised power system (Braxton and McLaughlin, 1990, 153).

In Morrison's novels the struggle to define and create a notion of selfhood in ways which are different from the stereotypical expectations of behaviour carried by the larger symbolic order as a whole inevitably involves a process of inner dislocation. As in, for example, *Song of Solomon*, this sense of inner disruption is sometimes resolved positively by the intervention of a female or androgynous figure in the central character's life. But this is not true of Morrison's first two novels where Pecola, suffering from a sense of self-loathing and false identity, retreats into schizophrenia after being raped by her father and where Sula withdraws into her grandmother's room to die alone and unfulfilled.

Although *The Bluest Eye* demonstrates Morrison's abiding interest, like that of many novelists, in dislocation, alienation, gaps and ellipses, these features arise out of the distortion of self created by the imposition of Euro-American cultural ideals on black people, including white concepts of beauty. Wilkerson (1988) has conveniently summarised three of the key characteristics of Morrison's narratives: they are rooted in arresting events (for example, a child having her father's baby, an insurance salesman attempting to fly off a roof, a First World War veteran announcing National Suicide Day, a slave mother killing her own child who later returns to haunt her); they involve personal histories which have been made tangled and complex; and they feature personal lives which skirt the edge of madness. However, whereas Wilkerson argues that the familiar in black folk lore is made strange in the telling, I would argue that in Morrison's work the eccentric (perhaps the ex-centric?) is often made explicable (or centred?). Both the first two novels are retrospective narratives: in *The Bluest Eye*, Claudia tries to understand her own involvement in Pecola's tragedy as the narrative also seeks to explain why a father in the ironically-named Breedlove family should impregnate his own daughter; in *Sula*, the people of a black neighbourhood, Medallion, retain and try to understand the implications for themselves and their community of the bizarre history and behaviour of the equally ironically named Peace family.

The explanation for many of the behaviours in the novel lies in the impact of prevailing white ideologies and dominant social structures on the black community, the negative consequences of which are inevitable as Claudia, partly in an attempt to abrogate her own responsibility, observes: 'This soil is bad for certain kinds of flowers. Certain seeds it will not nurture, certain fruit it will not bear . . .' (164). As we shall see, the authentic black self is buried so deep in some of the characters that their perceptions of themselves amount to self-hatred. This self-loathing is strongest in those characters who are farthest from their communities; for what they hate most is being different since difference brings abuse and cruelty. The self-hatred is often focused on the body as the most obvious indicator of race; hair and colour, for example, are recurrent concerns.

The black community is envisaged as existing like a cell within the larger white body of America, sustained by traditional strengths and values but being weakened by divisions within it. These divisions are the result of the gradual embourgeoisement of black people, as a consequence of a complicated process of adjustment and accommodation to white norms. In LeClair (1981), Morrison explains: 'The music kept us alive, but it's not enough any more. My people are being devoured'. The structure of *The Bluest Eye* is one of the means by which the novel explores how and why black people are being devoured and is best approached from this perspective. In speaking of African-Americans as being consumed, Morrison is inverting how whites, since earliest colonialist times, represented blacks as bestial. She is ironically adapting how African mythologies about slavery posited the whites as cannibals because blacks taken by them never returned; here perceiving the exploitation of blacks by whites as economic cannibalism. It is a view, however, which ignores how African-Americans have influenced language, dress, manners and culture in America, even in the South.

Not all critics have recognised the success of the novel in deconstructing the impact of white values on African-American people. Valerie Smith (1987) complains that *The Bluest Eye* does not 'address hard questions directly' (124); by this she means that it does not undertake to explain, for example, why black Americans aspire to unattainable standards of beauty. Her claims would seem to be borne out by Pecola's conclusion: 'There's really nothing more to say – except why. But since why is difficult to handle, one must take refuge in how'

(3). However, this is not the conclusion of the ostensibly omniscient narrator, but the view of Claudia as an adult trying to come to terms with her own role in Pecola's tragedy. What Claudia says does not suggest, as Smith argues, that the novel will take refuge in 'how'; it is a warning that what the narrative will uncover by means of explanation may be unpalatable.

The differences between the white and African-American cultures and between the sociopolitical contexts of the lives shaped within those cultures are pursued throughout *The Bluest Eye*, in the persistent contrasting of the Dick–Jane mythology of the primer with the Breedloves, the African-American family. The chapters which are introduced by lines from the primer extract, sometimes with a very subtle but significant variation, provide particularly bitter glosses on the bourgeois myth of the ideal family life. Each chapter enlarges on the Breedlove family while the themes are developed further with reference to a range of minor characters.

Black people are visible to whites in *The Bluest Eye* only in so far as they fit the white frame of society. The novel deconstructs this frame literally through dismembering the American Dick–Jane mythology: essential features of their world – house, family cat, mother, father, dog and friend – are separated from each other and their ideological significances probed through their inclusion and recontextualisation as plot elements in the Breedlove narrative. This process of dismemberment is analogous to Claudia's increasing dismemberment of a white doll in an attempt to discover the superiority of white culture:

> I fingered the face, wondering at the single-stroke eyebrows; picked at the pearly teeth stuck like two piano keys between red bowline lips. Traced the turned-up nose, poked the glassy blue eyeballs, twisted the yellow hair. I could not love it. But I could examine it to see what it was that all the world said was lovable. (14)

Claudia's destruction of the doll is a complex response which requires us to understand how Western culture, as McLaughlin explains, 'inspires hatred toward and among people of African descent, inducing destructive behaviours and an equally adverse disconnection from anything not western' (Braxton and McLaughlin, 1990, p. 170). In removing the various parts of the toy, Claudia dismantles the structure which constitutes and sustains it as an emblem of white beauty. Again, this is anticipated in the way in which the mythology of the primer is increasingly dismantled in the preface – the extract is reprinted, first without the punctuation and then with the spacing removed as well until all the letters run into each other. Claudia's obsession with discovering the source of the superiority of white culture leads her initially to torture the white girls whom the dolls represent but later to recoil in horror from this disinterested violence.

Within the ironic interplay of difference, the text dramatises and explores the consequences of enforced or voluntary abatement to white society, though in a sense no abatement can be entirely voluntary where black people exist in a world defined by the surrounding white society in terms of its blackness. Following Claudia's recollections of autumn 1940, in which she dismembers the white doll, the first chapter introduced by a primer extract develops the ironic differences between the pretty house of the primer and the abandoned store in which the Breedlove family lives. The store consists of rooms which have partitions that do not reach the ceiling; there is no bathroom but there is a toilet bowl which is out of sight though within earshot of the inhabitants. The irony is underscored by the repetition of the word 'pretty' which occurs only once in the preface and the way in which the extract breaks off, rather manically, with the first letter of that word.

The stress placed on the word 'pretty' also anticipates the misery endured by the Breedloves, and especially Pecola, in the following chapter because they believed they were ugly. That chapter is introduced with a primer extract that talks of family happiness and which breaks off equally significantly with the first letter of 'happy'. Unlike the ideal, sanitised family of Dick and Jane, the Breedlove's marriage is quarrelsome and violent, though both Pauline and Cholly Breedlove need this kind of relationship. Mrs Breedlove finds zest and passion in her formalised battles with her husband, whilst he projects on to her a sense of an innate inferiority arising from the way he has been treated by whites.

Whilst Claudia at this time dismembers the white doll in order to discover the nature of white superiority, Pecola regularly stares into her mirror 'trying to discover the secret of the ugliness, the ugliness that made her ignored or despised at school, by teachers and classmates alike' (34). The irony here is that the secret is not going to be found within herself, but within the culture that defines her as ugly. The focus of the novel is on the nature of whiteness: what Pecola sees in the eyes of the shopkeeper, Mr Yacobowski – 'the total absence of human recognition – the glazed separatenesss' – who as a white Jew should understand prejudice sufficiently to transcend it.

The world of the primer is very ordered and controlled as the short, tight sentences suggest, a world in which the middle-class, suburban home stands compartmentalised. Even the verbs are held in check – there are no adverbs and the sentences do not expand to embrace or convey the excitement of laughing or smiling or running; not even the dog's bark appears to interrupt this carefully constructed and ordered world. Claudia remembers the segregated Lake Shore Park for being well laid out and ordered, a quality embodied in the 'clean, white, well-behaved children and parents' (81). It has an illusory air to it which anticipates the interior of the 'proud' white house where Pauline becomes a servant. There its unreality for black people is conveyed in the details; the pink nighties, the embroidered pillow slips, the blue cornflowers in the top hems of the sheets, the 'fluffy' white towels and the 'cuddly' night clothes.

III

As we intimated at the outset, exploring the nature of whiteness in order to expose the negative consequences of the embourgeoisement of black culture gives *The Bluest Eye* a special slant. On one level, Geraldine, who has taken advantage of what little opportunity exists for black women from her background, is an example of a middle-class black woman who has become divorced from her African-American roots:

> They go to land-grant colleges, normal schools, and learn how to do the white man's work with refinement: home economics to prepare his food; teacher education to instruct black children in obedience; music to soothe the weary master and entertain his blunted soul. (64)

On another level, her history suggests that African-American women in her position surrender a deep-rooted passion which whites both envy and fear: 'The dreadful funkiness of passion, the funkiness of nature, the funkiness of the wide range of human emotions' (64). The word 'dreadful' here does not convey the views of the black kinswoman narrator but of the land-grant colleges which inculcate black students in white values.

In placing 'funk' at the centre of the African-American sensibility Morrison's text risks confirming a white stereotype of black women. But Geraldine's loss of passion is an indicator of the erosion of her black identity. Her physical being within the cultural frame she has adopted is described in terms of absences. The closest she comes to experiencing an orgasm is when her napkin slips free of her sanitary belt. In Geraldine's life the family kitten of the Dick–Jane mythology also becomes the object of displaced emotions. The cat, which she cradles in 'the deeply private areas of her lap', is the only thing to which she can show any kind of warmth. Geraldine's marriage is described as building a nest; it seems to consist only of ironed shirts and the phrase 'birthed Louis junior' suggests that parenthood, too, for her is a cold affair. Even the black cat which with blue eyes seems to signify the ideology to which Geraldine aspires, is as cold as an iceberg. The colours of Geraldine's home, of which we become aware when Junior invites Pecola in to torment her, are those of the primer; there is a red-and-gold Bible and lamps with green-and-gold bases. The word 'pretty' is strategically repeated throughout and the boy himself wears a white shirt and blue trousers.

Pecola disturbs Geraldine because she represents disorder: 'Hair uncombed, dresses falling apart, shoes untied and caked with dirt' (72), while the impact of white standardised concepts of beauty upon young women like Pecola is epitomised in the way in which the blue-eyed black cat when thrown at Pecola claws at her face. Geraldine's final words to Pecola pointedly recall Maureen's to Frieda and Claudia: 'Get out . . . You nasty little black bitch. Get out of my house' (72).

Instead of passing on ancestral wisdom, the traditional function of the African mother, a role assumed by Pilate in the later novel *Song of Solomon*, Geraldine passes on divisiveness. Ironically her son, Junior, would like to be accepted by the black boys; he would like to roll in the dirt with them and share their wildness, in effect overthrowing the control and order of the primer. Unable to do so, he takes his frustration out on brown-skinned girls as black men displace the humiliation which they suffer at the hands of whites on to their wives and children. Significantly he is also afraid of black girls who are said to hunt in packs. The animal metaphor, suggesting how *he* sees them not how the narrator perceives them, is an index of the extent to which Junior has assumed the derogatory white view of blacks as animals rather than people. The metaphor also suggests that there is defence in solidarity and highlights the vulnerability of those who try to go it alone. The image of the dead cat with its blue eyes closed, 'leaving only an empty, black, and helpless face' (71), suggests the cultural vacuum in which blacks who aspire to white norms may eventually find themselves.

The counterpoints to Geraldine in the novel are the three prostitutes: China, Poland and Miss Marie. Not only do they have a sexual autonomy which Geraldine has surrendered but they have economic independence. As such, they are also a counterpoint to other petty bourgeois African-Americans who benefit economically, socially and politically from the exploitation of their own people: the Peal family make money out of racial law suits while the Whitcombs exploit Africans who live in the West Indies.

The novel focuses not only on the interracial prejudices caused by the black petty bourgeoisie but also on the obsessive nature of their fixation with white values and the lengths to which they sometimes go to deny their blackness. The Whitcombs are so obsessed with not being black, grateful to the decaying British nobleman who gave them their whiteness, that they continue to intermarry to maintain it. Louis Junior's hair is deliberately cut short to hide its woolliness whilst his skin is lotioned to disguise its ashy Africanness. The most ironic example of all, however, is Maureen, the counterpoint to Pecola's humiliation and victimisation. Maureen looks and dresses like Jane, the archetypal Euro-American girl. Whilst Pecola is ignored by her teachers, Maureen is encouraged. Ironically, the lynch rope into which Maureen's hair is said to have been braided reminds us of slavery and oppression, the past on which black solidarity ought to be constructed. Here, a symbol of torture and death has been transformed into an adornment and robbed of its power. This kind of inversion is demonstrated also by the law suits which her parents issue for racism in order to make money, a perverse parody of the real struggles for civil rights.

The inner dislocation which the influence of white values creates in African-Americans, anticipating Pecola's eventual breakdown at the end of the novel, is embodied most obviously in the case of Pauline. In the movies which provide her with an escape from loneliness and alienation, Pauline encounters and assimilates a value system that classifies her and her family as ugly. The films present her with the white Dick–Jane mythology: 'White men taking such good care of they women, and they all dressed up in big clean houses with the bathtubs right in the same room with the toilet' (95). The line from the primer which introduces this chapter concerns how 'nice' the white mother is and how much she laughs. It is anticipated and contradicted by Claudia's own recollections of spring in the preceding chapter. Although she doesn't hate her mother for it, her memories of the season are shot through with recollections of the sting left by beatings from thin, green and supple twigs. Green was one of the cheerful colours of the house in the primer extract, but for Claudia, the colour, like the season, brings no cheer; it caused her to miss the 'steady stroke of a strap or the firm but honest slap of a hairbrush' (75). Ironically, it is the way in which the white myths create an inner dislocation within Pauline Williams that causes her to be less than 'nice' with her own daughter. In the white home in which she becomes a servant she finds an order and beauty that causes her to deny her own family and especially her daughter. When Pecola, her daughter, inadvertently enters the white home and frightens the 'little pink-and-yellow girl', Pauline punishes her and comforts the white girl. Pauline has moved with her husband to a community that is more obviously white than that from which she came. Her schizophrenia is a product of the enforced isolation, exaggerated by the way in which the other black women she meets are amused by her for not straightening her hair, as they have done in imitation of white women, and for retaining the dialect of the South. The novel contrasts not only the isolation of the white, nuclear family with the community of the South – evidenced in the attention Aunt Jimmy receives from her neighbours during her illness and in the community gathering at her funeral – but the isolation of the African-American in the North.

Even though Pauline's marriage collapses into a cycle of violence and unsatisfying sex, she refuses to leave Cholly for the white woman and a romanticised concept of 'sisterhood'. For Pauline race becomes more important than gender: 'But later on it didn't seem none too bright for a black woman to leave a black man for a white woman' (93). As becomes clear from the monologues which betray the complexity of her situation, her experience of how white doctors treat white women differently from black women is crucial to her rejection of the white concept of 'sisterhood'. Once again, the point is made that cultural dislocation, as for Geraldine, brings about an emotional and sexual dislocation. The implication that her white employee has married a man with 'a slash in his face instead of a mouth' (94), is that she has never experienced the passion which Pauline used to find with Cholly, encapsulated in the description of orgasm from a woman's point of view:

> I begin to feel those little bits of color floating up into me – deep in me. That streak of green from the june-bug light, the purple from the berries trickling along my thighs, Mama's lemonade yellow runs sweet in me. Then I feel like I'm laughing between my legs, and the laughing gets all mixed up with the colors, and I'm afraid I'll come and I'm afraid I won't. But I know I will. And I do. And it be rainbow all inside. And it lasts and lasts and lasts . . . (101–2)

IV

The order of the white world, its coherence and moral certainty, is juxtaposed throughout with the disunity and search for coherence in the lives of the African-Americans. The chapter which contrasts the white, mythical mother of the primer with Pauline is followed by a chapter that takes up the description of the father as big, strong and protective in the primer extract. This is itself ironic in the light of the text's subsequent celebration of the inner strength and fortitude not of black fathers but of black women:

> Everybody in the world was in a position to give them orders. White women said, 'Do this.' White children said, 'Give me that.' White men said, 'Come here.' Black men said, 'Lay down.' The only people they need not take orders from were black children and each other. But they took all of that and re-created it in their own image. . . . They patted biscuits into flaky ovals of innocence – and shrouded the dead. They plowed all day and came home to nestle like plums under the limbs of their men. (108)

The chapter, in contrasting Cholly with the strong, protective father of the primer, begins by fleshing out his past and concludes with his rape of his own daughter, an incident which can only be understood, if not excused, in the light of this background. Compounding the irony, the primer extract begins by asking the white father if he will 'play' with his daughter, Jane, a verb which in the Breedlove episode acquires a much less innocent connotation. There is a further irony in the way in

which Claudia's recollections are of Frieda relating how her father beat
up Mr Henry because he touched her breasts and of being dragged to
the doctor by her mother in case she had been 'ruined'. Within this
account, Cholly is remembered not for being a strong, protective
father but for being always drunk. As Hernton observes, it is
concomitant with the black literary heritage that black women write
about the violence and abuse which they have suffered at the hands of
black men (Braxton and McLaughlin, 1990, 209). This has created
problems, however, for black women writers. When they document the
violence and rape they have suffered, even as young girls, they are
sometimes accused of sowing the seeds of division in what should be
perceived of as a homogeneous community in the face of white
oppression. As Hernton says, 'one of the most galvanizing examples of
this is the hostility black men have toward Toni Morrison' (202). This
makes it all the more important to understand the complexity of what
Morrison is trying to do.

In *The Bluest Eye*, the white father of the primer is invoked as a
contrast not only to Cholly but to Cholly's own father who abandoned
him to his mother. The way in which the text returns to Cholly's past to
contextualise what has happened is a device used in several of
Morrison's novels to illustrate and explore how what appears to be
immoral behaviour is actually the result of the unnatural experiences
imposed on black people by whites. The opening sentence of this
chapter sharply contrasts Cholly's childhood with the way in which
Pauline's white charges have been brought up; he was left on a junk
heap wrapped in two blankets and an old newspaper. This rejection is
compounded by some of his later experiences. His grandmother takes
him to her bed for warmth in winter, an act which the reference to the
way in which he could see her wrinkled, sagging breasts suggests is
unnatural, and it is with her that he witnesses violence for the first time
when she takes a razor strap to his mother. Here the novel is not only
concerned with the way in which Cholly's relationship with his father
has been obliterated, but with the way in which white racism and
colonialism fractured relationships between mother and child, an
increasing and recurring theme in Morrison's work as we shall see in
discussions of her subsequent novels. At the beginning of her final
narrated section, the adult Claudia recalls her mother as she was in
1929, so that her newfound appreciation of her black identity and of
how Pecola's tragedy involved them all is concomitant with a renewal
of her bond with her female ancestral line. After she has been raped by

her father, Pecola lies on the kitchen floor trying to connect the pain between her legs with the face of her mother looming over her. The connection is complex, but it is one that the reader as much as Pecola has to make through the way in which Pauline denied her daughter the mother/daughter bonding which in Morrison's novels, as we shall see in the discussion of *Beloved,* is crucial to black women's self-definition.

Cholly's rape of his daughter is as much rooted in the past as in the present. His young daughter's helpless presence arouses a range of emotions within him, culminating before the rape in a hatred reminiscent of that which years earlier he had transferred to Darlene when the white hunters forced him to 'perform' sexually with her in front of them. Pecola's innocent gesture of scratching the back of her leg with her foot reminds him of the first occasion he was aroused by Pauline. The whole episode is shot through with confusion: between memories of Pauline and the excitement of what is forbidden; between the past with Darlene and the present with Pecola; between desire for Pecola and tenderness for her. When Cholly approaches his daughter he does so crawling on all fours like a child or the animal which whites have made him feel. Nibbling the back of her leg he regresses into the most primal of experiences, while his closed eyes suggest how he is unable to see the full moral implications of what he is doing. Right up until the act of penetration, though, he retains some semblance of moral being, albeit confused, wanting to 'fuck her – tenderly' (128). When he enters and impregnates her, the text makes clear that all moral responsibility and familial dignity have been abandoned: 'His soul seemed to slip down to his guts . . .' After he has finished, he stands at the end of the chapter as a pathetic figure made limp, as the sight of Pecola's 'grayish panties' emphasises, as much by the realisation of what he has done as by his ejaculation. Yet he is also a tragic figure broken, as the final references to his hatred make clear, by what white society has done to him and this is reinforced by the way the account of his rape of Pecola brings the incident with Darlene in the woods to mind. When he and Darlene began to make love together, she tickled his ribs and grabbed his ribcage while he dug his fingers into the neck of her dress; his assault on Pecola begins in earnest when he digs his fingers into her waist. The description of how his soul had fallen down to his guts recalls how the flashlight of the white hunters, forcing him to penetrate Darlene, 'wormed its way into his guts' (116) while 'the gigantic thrust' he makes into his daughter reminds us of how with

Darlene 'he almost wished he could do it – hard, long, and painfully . . .'

The women who gossip about the rape perpetrate the contempt which led to it. The novel comes full circle from its initial questioning of the mode of perception that labels some plants flowers and others weeds. Claudia conjures up an image of Pecola's child that is not ugly, as the gossips suggest, but a counterpoint to the white doll of the beginning and to Pauline's pink-white charges: 'It was in a dark, wet place, its head covered with great O's of wool, the black face holding like nickels, two clean black eyes, the flared nose, kissing-thick lips, and the living, breathing silk of black skin' (149). Claudia's memory of Pecola's victimisation by so many people anticipates the ironic juxtaposition of the primer excerpt which introduces Pecola's schizophrenia and which focuses on the friend who will play with Jane. Of course the effect of this is to underscore Pecola's loneliness and lack of friends.

The Bluest Eye is an innovative novel in which its experiments with form are determined by the perspectives and approaches which it brings to the condition of the African-American at the tense interface between two cultures. One of these perspectives is the way in which language is enmeshed with power structures, pursued throughout the novel by the persistent contrasting of the Dick–Jane mythology of the primer with the Breedlove family. Within this ironic interplay of difference, the text brings a particular perspective not only to the impact of white ideologies on the black community, but also to the nature of whiteness and its inappropriateness to determine the contours of African-American culture and lived experience.

3
Sula (1973)

Both *The Bluest Eye* and *Sula* involve an incident in which a gang of bullies is defeated. The difference between the two respective episodes is indicative of the difference between the two novels. In *The Bluest Eye*, the threat posed by the bullies draws Claudia, Frieda, Pecola and Maureen together until Claudia and Frieda become unable to forgive the lighter-skinned Maureen for assuming white standards of physical beauty which they envy. Maureen's subsequent articulation of her contempt of their black skin, in which blackness and ugliness are perceived as synonymous, in turn epitomises the central concern of the novel with how black culture is being destroyed by the impact of white norms upon it. In *Sula*, the threat posed by the gang to Sula and Nel brings out Sula's reserves of strength and her unpredictability which help focus the novel's concern with these elements. Sula's response also provides a further example of behaviour in the novel which is explicable in terms of an African rather than an American model of self.

Toni Morrison's second novel, like her first, is written within an innovative but finely crafted narrative framework. As we have seen, *The Bluest Eye* uses an extract from an American primer as its preface and throughout contrasts the white family of the primer with a black family. The novel is divided into four sections narrated by Claudia MacTeer looking back on her childhood in which she was involved in the tragic disintegration of a victimised black girl. Within each section there are further subsections narrated by an omniscient narrator and introduced by lines from the primer extract in the preface in order to pursue an ironic interplay of difference throughout. *Sula*, which focuses on the friendship between two black women, is divided into two parts. In the first part, Sula and Nel become childhood friends in a black community and together become involved in the death of a young boy; in part two, Sula returns to the community as an adult after a ten-year absence which is never satisfactorily explained. Each part in a number of ways is an inverse mirror image of the other. Characters introduced and developed in part one are reintroduced in inverse order in the second part and the novel opens and closes with an act of memory. There are ten chapters, each located in a specific year – 1919, 1920, 1921, 1922, 1927, 1937, 1939, 1940, 1941, 1965 – and, from even a cursory glance at this span of years, it is quite clear that the novel, like *The Bluest Eye*, is fragmentary and elliptical. Indeed the centre of the novel is literally a blank, a missing decade when the reader knows very little of what happened to Sula. There are other examples of lacunae in the novel, too, such as the sudden departure of Eva, Sula's grandmother, in 1921, ostensibly leaving all her children with Mrs Suggs for a day but returning eighteen months later with an amputated leg for which again no plausible explanation is offered.

II

The prologue, describing the redevelopment of the black neighbourhood in a small Ohio town by white property interests and the exploitation of black people by whites, might lead the reader to expect that this novel, like *The Bluest Eye*, is about black people being consumed by the surrounding white society. Both novels are concerned with the way in which the geography of an area shapes and is shaped by its sociospatial politics, but *Sula* places more emphasis on the ability of the propertied classes to change the geography of an area in line with their own interests. The prologue to *Sula* points out that the black neighbourhood is called 'the suburbs now, but when black people lived there it was called the Bottoms' (3). This linguistic shift emphasises how language can be and has been manipulated by those in authority to maintain their advantage and protect their positions, a concern developed in all Morrison's work. In the prologue to *Sula*, this issue is developed in the story of the 'good white farmer' who dupes his freed slave into accepting land in the hills, 'the bottom of heaven'. In adapting the proverbial folk anecdote, a staple technique of traditional African writing for communicating ancestral wisdom, Morrison compounds the irony of the prologue that black people have the higher ground in so far as they hold the higher moral ground. This moral position is more forcefully delineated in *Sula* than in *The Bluest Eye*, giving the prologue's account of the black neighbourhood, despite its portrayal of the hardship and poverty, an upbeat confidence which borders on the sentimental:

> just a neighborhood where on quiet days people in valley houses could hear singing sometimes, banjos sometimes, and, if a valley man happened to have business up in those hills – collecting rent or insurance payments – he might see a dark woman in a flowered dress doing a bit of cakewalk . . . (4)

Against this strong realisation that African-Americans hold the high moral ground, Morrison also develops the prologue's concern with geopolitical and linguistic boundaries in new but concomitant directions from those followed in her earlier novel. They are first developed through the portrayal of Shadrack, a First World War veteran driven mad by the horrors of the trenches. There are two interrelated perspectives in the narrative's treatment of Shadrack, each of which serves to focus larger themes of the novel: his struggle to order and focus experience, 'making a place for fear as a way of controlling it', and the people's attempt to come to terms with him; once they 'understood the boundaries and nature of his madness, they could fix him, so to speak, into the scheme of things' (14). Here the novel anchors several perspectives on the black experience. Firstly, the difficulty that the black members of the community have in coming to terms with Shadrack is indicative of their displacement. As Vashti Lewis (Braxton and McLaughlin, 1990, 321) points out, in traditional African culture Shadrack would have been treated with awe and respect. Shadrack's divine nature arises from his state of unconsciousness as a victim of shell shock. In traditional African ontology the spirit of people who lay unconscious for many days left the body and entered the ancestral world (Braxton and McLaughlin, 1990, 316). The inability of the community of Medallion to incorporate Shadrack anticipates the way in which they are unable to deal with the adult Sula. Secondly, Shadrack focuses the concern of black people to try to place what has happened, and is happening to them, into their scheme of things. Shadrack's disorientation is resonant of that of African-Americans in twentieth-century America: 'Twenty-two years old, weak, hot, frightened, not daring to acknowledge the fact that he didn't even know who or what he was . . . with no past, no language, no tribe, no source, . . .' (12). The way in which Shadrak's tin plate is divided – 'reassured that the white, the red and the brown would stay where they were – would not explode or burst forth from their restricted zones' (8) – epitomises the precarious nature of the white geopolitical structures and the Western philosophical system of ordering, dividing and classifying.

The focus of the novel is upon the black community which exists behind and transcends the white boundaries which have tried to define and contain it and through which self-centredness, or what the novel calls 'me-ness', sends shock waves. Although Toni Morrison is interested in notions of community, solidarity and ancestry, her novels frequently enter these subjects through examples of dislocation and disunity and move towards an affirmation of communal values. The deliberateness of this technique is evident from her essay 'City Limits, Village Values: Concepts of the Neighbourhood in Black Fiction' where she argues:

> While individualism and escape from the community was frequently a major theme in Black writing, it should be regarded for what it was: 'A devotion to self-assertion can be a devotion to discovering distinctive ways of expressing community values, social purpose, mutual regard or . . . affirming a collective experience.' (Jaye and Watts, 1981, 38)

Morrison's assertion of community over individualism displays the African roots of her work for in indigenous African society an individual acting in isolation or heroically outside of the community is not respected: 'When a character defies a village law or shows contempt for its values, it may be seen as a triumph to white readers, while Blacks may see it as an outrage' (ibid.).

The affirmation of community values, social purpose and mutual regard is evident throughout *Sula*; positively in, for example, the way in which the Suggs help Eva, and negatively, towards the end of the novel, in the way in which Sula dies alone and unloved. Her isolation in the novel is underscored by the way in which her mother and grandmother, Hannah and Eva, are absorbed into the community despite their anomalies. Indeed, as Lewis observes, in the African Babangi language the possible meanings of the name, Sula, include to alter from a proper condition to a worse one and to fail in spirit (Braxton and McLaughlin, 1990, 316). Sula's failure in spirit is emphasised after her death through the preparation of her body by whites instead of by blacks and through Nel's solitary black presence at the internment though members of the black community appear after the whites have gone, the significance of which we shall return to later. Here, as in the previous novel, the behaviours of individuals within the black community are made complex and problematic by its unnatural relationship to an engulfing white society. Nel's 'me-ness' develops only after seeing her mother Helene's experience of being black in the larger white society. In describing these experiences, the narrative focuses on Helene as the main protagonist, but also upon the way the child, Nel, interprets and internalises what happens to her mother and how she responds. Eventually the narrative voice and Nel's perspective become virtually indistinguishable: 'Like a street pup that wags its tail at the very doorjamb of the butcher shop he has been kicked away from only moments before, Helene smiled. Smiled dazzlingly and coquettishly at the salmon-colored face of the conductor' (21).

The name Wright suggests not only conformity to socially-accepted values and codes of behaviour, but, if we ignore the 'r' instead of the 'w', conformity to white norms. Her mother was the child of a creole whore but was brought up by her grandmother to deny 'her mother's wild blood' in an environment which drove her 'imagination under-ground'. Married to Wiley Wright, Helene lived in a house which resembles that in the Dick–Jane mythology in *The Bluest Eye*: 'a lovely house with a brick porch and real lace curtains at the window' (18). Helene is proud of how far she has climbed socially; unable to find a Catholic Church in Medallion, she has been brought up under a 'multi-colored Virgin Mary', she worships in the most 'conservative' black church she can find. Other blacks who are in many respects white and deny their blackness – the uniformed black men Nel sees on the train and the figure of Pretty Johnnie whom Eva classes as all white because he has no blood – act as commentaries on Helene. To a white reader versed in European literature, Sula Peace and Nel Wright may appear as a pair of binary opposites. Sula, ironically named Peace, is the more rebellious and upsets the black community while Nel marries and settles down within it. However, the narrative resists interpretations based on binary oppositions and in doing so suggests that the Western philosophical tradition founded on binary opposites can act as a straitjacket on thought. As McDowell points out, the novel frequently 'forces us to question our readings, to hold our judgement in check, and to continually revise it' (McKay, 1988, 86).

In creating characters who defy received assumptions about how black women should behave, Morrison confronts the larger problem facing African-American women writers which we mentioned in the introduction: a legacy in which black women are either idealised or portrayed negatively. Elleke Boehmer argues, African literature in the past 'has constituted a nationalist and patriarchal preserve' (Nasta, 1991, 9). Women are often seen as the idealised bearers of the nation's children, often sons, while 'men have monopolised the field of nationalist identity and self-image'. As Krumholz (1993) observes: 'In *Sula*, Morrison both cherishes and criticizes the character Nel, who (ambiguously) embodies the myth of the black woman as a nurturing, self-sacrificing, infinitely strong burden bearer' (554). Some writers such as Alice Walker have tried to develop positive self-images for their black women characters by repossessing matriarchal myths, especially the Africa/Goddess/Mother mythology, but as Boehmer points out, there is a difficulty here because these matriarchal myths cannot be easily separated from those which support patriarchal authority. Morrison resists subscribing to such unitary icons and develops more dispersed and multifarious concepts of self. As Boehmer drawing upon Kristeva observes, 'Writing is "transformative", operating through the displacement of what is already signified, bringing forth the not-yet-imagined and the transgressive' (Nasta, 1991, 10).

Boehmer's point helps us to take further Koenen's (1985) argument in relation to Morrison's works themselves that in her black, female-headed households women survive by 'self-inventing' (McKay, 1988, 199). The realisation and articulation of the not-yet-imagined acquires particular importance for many black women because their quest for identity, as we said earlier, often begins with a negative definition which they must overcome; a definition compounded, as is demonstrated in *The Bluest Eye*, by the way in which black men discharge their frustrations on to black women. In addition, as Suarez observes, discussing the work of the Black British writer, Joan Riley, 'to the absence of an authentic black and female self, we must add the absence of place, of belonging, the absence of an authentic motherland' (Nasta, 1991, 229). de Weever (1991) is critical of Morrison's response to this dilemma, arguing that in Morrison's novels 'it is not the men who develop a feeling, feminine side, but the women who develop male attributes' (31). The exception to de Weever's observation, of course, is Paul D in *Beloved* whom we will discuss in a later chapter, but she does identify several shared aspects of the way in which three of Morrison's female characters – Sula and Pilate in *Song of Solomon*, and Jadine in *Tar Baby* – realise the 'not-yet-imagined': their sense of owning themselves; the way they work out their own destinies; the freedom and sense of adventure they show in seeking to satisfy their own wants, needs and desires (32). The extent to which Sula is ready to create her own notion of selfhood is emphasised by the birth imagery with which she is associated; by the tadpole, for example, which Shadrack thinks he observes in her birthmark and by the foetal position in which she dies.

III

Of all the characters in the novel, Sula herself most obviously defies a stable and unified reading; there are moments, as Valerie Smith (1987) points out, when the text seems to validate Sula's way of life (130). Yet as another critic, Robert Grant, has noted, the reader struggles 'to "conceive" of such a character whose candour and awareness are alternately admirable, alienating, humorous and a little frightening' (McKay, 1988, 98). Sula, like Nel, is described in her youth as having a 'mercury mood' and is 'skittish, frightened and bold – all at the same time' (56). But she needs to be seen within the context of African literary traditions as much as European ones. In the European literary tradition, largely under the influence of the binary opposition within European religion, there is often a clear distinction between good and evil characters. However, in much African literature, good and evil coexist within each individual and are subject to an ongoing process of negotiation. This is characteristic of the trickster figure, which Gates, Jr (1984) observes occurs in many black oral narratives from different parts of the world. The trickster, as Radin (1956) points out, is 'the undifferentiated present within every individual', 'the promise of God and man', and is 'he who was before good and evil, denier, affirmer, destroyer and creator' (168–9).

Western thought, as the European literary theorist and philosopher Derrida recognised, is also characterised by a tendency to construct a hierarchy of values: for example, reason over imagination; mind over body; work over leisure. In *Sula*, this hierarchy, like the traditional binary opposition of good and evil, is resisted by the nature of the novel itself. As Wilkerson (1988) observes without offering an explanation, this novel 'is moved through dialogue and the narrative restricted to moments of silence' (188). In *Sula* Morrison's frequent avoidance of a judgemental narrative voice in favour of a documentary mode where judgement is implicit rather than explicit, promotes a view of Medallion as a kaleidoscope of different behaviours and viewpoints which are constantly being negotiated. The initial difficulty with Sula and Nel is their failure, if not refusal, to discriminate from the whirlpool of life around them: 'And they had no priorities. They could be distracted from watching a fight with mean razors by the generous smell of hot tar being poured by roadmen two hundred yards away' (55). Of course there are values and hierarchies within the community but these are fluid, as the description of the community's behaviour at Nel Wright's wedding suggests, where 'the church women who frowned on any bodily expression of joy (except when the hand of god commanded it) tapped their feet' and 'even Helene Wright had mellowed with the cane' (79). The background details of Medallion – the razor fights, the doctoring of the punch at Nel's wedding, the women fighting over Ajax – reinforce the volatility of the community, epitomised in the main events of the narrative, which is itself partly a product of rapid urbanisation in which clear conventions of behaviour have not been developed. The volatile nature of the major characters and their unpredictability are reinforced by the minor characters such as the Deweys who, described as 'mischievous, cunning, private and completely unhousebroken' (84–5), mirror Sula and Nel who, as youngsters, are described as 'skittish, frightened and bold – all at the same time' while 'barefoot looking for mischief' (56). Behind this conflict within the community, however, there is a strong impulse toward harmony and balance of which Sula herself makes us aware through her name, Peace, and through the robins – birds traditionally associated with peace – which accompany her return to Medallion.

What is particularly disturbing about Sula, and also Nel to a lesser extent, is that the negotiation across a kaleidoscope of different, potential behaviours occurs increasingly at a solipsistic level which is hinted at, again in a documentary style, early in the book: 'In the safe harbor of each other's company they could afford to abandon the ways of other people and concentrate on their own perception of things' (55). The blanket under which Nel removes the clothes pin from her nose symbolises the solipsism and secrecy into which she is lured by Sula. The voice of authorial judgement intrudes into the documentary at the point where Sula and Nel are described as having substituted detached observation for the active, albeit at times volatile, participation which sustains the community: 'Joined in mutual admiration they watched each day as though it were a movie arranged for their amusement' (55). Not only does the word 'amusement' here undermine the intensity of the emotional and material struggle of most people's lives in Medallion, but it contradicts the way in which the constant references to time, to the seasons and to external events in the narrative make clear that nothing is organised for any one particular individual.

McDowell has drawn attention to how *Sula* defies the assumption of a self that is knowable, centred and unified and posits instead a view of the self as multiple, fluid and relational (McKay, 1988, 81). This is reinforced in the book by the changing nature of Sula's birthmark: to Nel it is a stemmed rose; to Jude, a copper head and a rattlesnake; to Shadrack, a tadpole. Moreover throughout the novel Sula is associated with water and fluidity even to the extent that some critics have labelled her a water spirit. The model of the self from African literature is more fluid than those which have been developed in the Hebraic-Christian West. In the African model, individuals are obliged to negotiate constantly different possibilities of behaviour within themselves and this gives a particular significance to the trickster figure in African and African-American writing to which Sula is connected without necessarily being a trickster in the traditional sense herself. Although acknowledging that we should approach Sula from the perspectives provided by traditional African culture and African cosmology, Lewis's suggestion that Sula is a water spirit or priestess does not do justice to her volatility and to the challenge which she frequently presents in the way her association with the trickster figure would (Braxton and McLaughlin, 1990, 320).

The trickster, according to Gates, Jr (1984), is normally male and characterised by 'individuality, satire, parody, irony, magic, indeterminacy, open-endedness, ambiguity, sexuality, chance, uncertainty, disruption and reconciliation, betrayal and loyalty, closure and disclosure, encasement and rupture' (6). Although at times he can be like any other citizen or tribal member, he is essentially an amoral being who flouts the most sacred taboos with impunity. The trickster occurs so widely in black literature that there are many variations, but with commonly recurring characteristics: he is always a wanderer, representative of disruption and disorder, sometimes to the point of anarchy, and usually oversexed. As in Sula's case, his outrageous behaviour finally alienates all his fellows and he is left alone as an outcast from society. Such tricksters abound in folktales: for example, the medieval French story of Reynard the Fox or the African-American

story of Brer Rabbit, the linchpin of Morrison's novel *Tar Baby* which
we will discuss later. But similar characters are also found in classical
literature, modern European literature, Victorian literature and
American literature from the Spanish picaro, such as Lazarillo de
Tormes, to Patrick McMurphy of Ken Kesey's *One Flew Over the
Cuckoo's Nest*.

The fluid model of self which we have identified as a characteristic of
the trickster, acknowledging 'the undifferentiated present within every
individual', directs us to the issue of unpredictability – the element that
makes individuals and individual relationships in Medallion volatile,
dramatic and interesting. Sula is alive to the unpredictability within
her; Helene, like the white people she emulates, is not. When Sula
returns to Medallion, she brings unpredictability back into Nel's life.
Once again Shadrack analogises a key theme in the novel because his
fears of death and the First World War battlefield are inexplicable and
unpredictable. He invents National Suicide Day in order to contain and
control his fear: '. . . if one day a year were devoted to it [death],
everybody could get it out of the way and the rest of the year would be
safe and free' (14). Of course there is an innate human need to try to
control the unexpected: Eva, after all, reflects that she might have been
prepared for Hannah's death had she read the omens. But Shadrack's
scheme is built upon a grand illusion; the rest of the year would never
be 'safe and free'. Life is unpredictable and people are mercurial as
Hannah's death and the return of Sula suggest. The contrast between
Sula's and Nel's upbringing emphasises the dangers in denying this.

IV

At first Sula's unpredictability is exciting and disturbing, as, for
example, when she slices off the tip of her finger as a warning to the
white bullies. The gesture is disturbing not because it is a desperate act,
not only because it implies the threat of castration as does Sula's later
nailfile and knives fantasy about Ajax, but because it appears to be so
calculating. The reader is not told what Sula is thinking; only her
actions are described and in such careful detail that we suspect they
mirror the slow deliberation of her mind. In the description of Sula and
Nel's peeling of the twig, the author's apparent silence and the
apparent lack of authorial intervention in the documentary compounds
the disturbing silence of the two girls working together and copying

each other. Significantly Nel's copying of Sula in tracing the intricate patterns suggests that Sula's is the more complex of the two psyches. But the relationship between the two girls is as fluid and complicated as that between good and evil within the individual. Nel, after all, does take the initiative at times; it is she who thinks to strip the twig to its 'smoothy, creamy innocence' and tears up the rooted grass (58). The fact that the two holes which they dig are the same suggests that they should not be seen in binary opposition to each other. In the course of the novel, however, Sula eventually becomes the more disturbing and disturbed of the two. The narrative's ambiguity over, for example, why Sula watched her own mother burn to death – whether it was out of a perverse curiosity or because she was struck motionless and speechless through shock – continues to subvert the attachment of unitary meanings to Sula.

In the account of the response of the two girls at Chicken Little's funeral service, where the ceremony designed to bring the community together can only emphasise their disjunction, the narrative provides explicit insight into Nel's thoughts – 'although she knew she had "done nothing", she felt convicted and hanged right there in the pew' – but not into Sula's psyche. Indeed the documentary approach at this point draws attention to its failure to provide the same level of insight in Sula's case as in Nel's: 'Sula simply cried. Soundlessly and with no heaving and gasping for breath, she let the tears roll into her mouth and slide down her chin to dot the front of her dress' (65). The disturbance created by the lack of insight into her mind is compounded by the way in which the tears appear to be detached from Sula herself.

In part one of the novel, Sula's behaviour, however volatile, is contextualised within the mercurial nature of the community as a whole and of particular individuals. In part two, an older Sula, accomplished and relatively wealthy, is set apart from Medallion. Ultimately, towards the end of the novel, she is buried by whites. Members of the black community come to the graveyard in a final attempt to deal with her as a community, to integrate her into the community's experience, as the hymn – 'Shall We Gather At The River' – suggests. The question which the hymn poses hangs not only over Sula and her relationship with the community, but over the disrupted community's own prospect of survival.

In exposing the disruptive dialectic between Sula and the community, the narrative maintains the ambiguity of part one. For example, Sula's return is accompanied, as we observed earlier, by a

plague of robins, ironically because traditionally they are birds of
harmony and unity. But Eva suggests that this may be more of an omen
than a coincidence. In the Bible and in African literature a plague is a
visit of judgement on a people. In traditional African literature the
plague can often only be lifted by a sacrifice on the part of the
community itself; after Sula's death Shadrack leads the people in the
last National Suicide Day celebration and many of them are killed in
the accident at the tunnel. When Sula accuses Eva of placing her leg on
the railway line to claim compensation from the insurance, Eva's denial
only means that the reader can never be sure whether the allegation is
true or false. The ambiguity in the second part of the novel, however,
appears to work towards a different goal from that in the first part and
it is one of the techniques used in turning Sula into something of the
trickster figure of African mythology. From the moment of her return,
as Eva points out, Sula proves disruptive: 'You ain't been in this house
ten seconds already you starting something' (92). One of the salient
features of the trickster figure is the way the onus of interpretation is
placed upon the observer. When Sula returns to Medallion, she is being
constantly interpreted by those who meet her, especially Eva, and in
this point of focalisation by the reader. Sula's statement of intention – 'I
don't want to make somebody else. I want to make myself' (92) – may
seem reasonable given the negative definitions from which black
women have to start. But it also expresses an individuality which
challenges traditional African regard for community values, hence
Eva's immediate angry response. This negative interpretation of Sula's
desire to make herself is reinforced by the way in which Sula turns her
buttocks toward Eva, both physically and metaphorically: 'And I'll split
this town in two and everything in it . . .' (93). Sula becomes increasingly
disturbing and disturbed until she threatens to set fire to Eva. But, in
keeping with the trickster tradition, even this threat is ambivalent; it
may be a serious threat or an off-the-cuff remark in the heat of the
moment. Just as the narrative of Sula slicing off the tip of her finger
might suggest her own scheming behaviour, the description of her
assumption of the role of Eva's guardian might suggest her own careful,
scheming attention to detail. Once again, the ambiguity is compounded
by the narrative's silence on the matter. Here, however, the ambiguity
is heightened by the silence over much of the missing decade in Sula's
life which precedes part two. This is the reverse of the situation in the
later novel, *Tar Baby* (1981), where Son's eight homeless years provide
an explanation for his eccentric behaviour. Once again the narrative of

Sula ·draws attention to its own silence as Nel challenges Sula: 'You wasn't in no college for – what – ten years now?' (99).

The most explicit definition of Sula as a trickster comes from Nel: 'Her old friend had come home. Sula. Who had made her laugh, who made her see old things with new eyes . . .' (95). Making someone see things differently is one of the key elements of the trickster, but Sula's role is rooted in a decade of which Nel and the reader are never fully informed so that Nel's thought of the return of her old friend ironically raises the question to what extent is Sula the same old friend whom Nel thinks she remembers. Nel's assessment of Sula as enabling people to 'see old things with new eyes' is given a sinister interpretation by Jude who reckons she has 'an odd way of looking at things' when the black mark over her eye is significantly likened to a rattlesnake (104).

Radin (1956) points out that the trickster figure is 'at one and the same time creator and destroyer . . . he possesses no values, moral or social, is at the mercy of his passions and appetites, yet through his actions all values come into being' (ix). Sula presents a moral challenge to the community which the community, commensurate with African tradition, must resolve as a community. She destabilises the impulse toward harmony which lies behind the unpredictability and volatile nature of life in Medallion. Her behaviour on one level may appear to expose the hypocrisy of the community: 'Later, when they saw how she took Jude, then ditched him for the others, and heard how he bought a bus ticket to Detroit (where he bought but never mailed birthday cards to his sons), they forgot all about Hannah's easy ways (or their own) and said she was a bitch' (112). However, this would be too simplistic an interpretation. The use of the third person plural in the narrative suggests that the community is more homogeneous than it is in practice, denying its kaleidoscope of heterogeneous elements. Moreover, it is not merely that its members, and especially the men, are hypocritical. They forget temporarily the ongoing process of negotiation between possible behaviours which determines the extent to which individuals act in their own interests or in the interests of the collective.

Through the portrayal of Sula, the narrative exposes a pursuit of individuality similar to the kind which, as with Geraldine in *The Bluest Eye* and Hannah in *Sula*, can lead black people to reject their blackness in favour of assimilation to the norms of the host society. Sula's mark which in the beginning of the novel is a stemmed rose, suggesting individual fulfilment and rootedness, eventually becomes ashes, suggesting the potential dissolution not only of herself but of black cultural identity in general: 'She had no center, no speck around which to grow' (119). This is realised in the final chapter of the book which takes the reader forwards, 24 years after Sula's death, to a year just before that from which the prelude was written, for here, unlike in the prelude, the golf course is only a rumour. The chapter begins with an ironic statement – 'Things were so much better in 1965' – which it then deconstructs and undermines. The narrator's voice merges with the observations of Nel in order to lament the passing of community: 'Now there weren't any places left, just separate houses with separate televisions and separate telephones and less and less dropping by . . .' (166). The construction of the language changes as it describes the development; not only is the word 'separate' strategically repeated to stress the new emphasis upon privacy and individuality but the repetition of 'and' gives the impression of a fragmented rather than an integrated space. Two examples of change – the emergence of a new type of prostitute and the tendency to put the old people into residential homes – epitomise not only the loss of community, but the extent to which black people are becoming increasingly assimilated into white norms and values. The new prostitutes who operate in diverse economic contexts are 'pale and dull' having lost the 'funkiness' which Morrison, as we saw earlier, identifies with black women; the increasing reliance upon residential homes for the elderly suggests how issues such as old age are no longer seen as 'community' but as 'individual' problems. Nel's sorrow at the end of the novel is intense and deep but there is no community to sing it out as at the funeral of Chicken Little or at the death of Hannah where the women who prepare her body for burial weep for her 'burned hair and wrinkled breasts as though they themselves had been lovers' (27). Sula's crying for Chicken Little anticipates Nel's weeping for her at the end of the novel for though the tears roll, it is too much an internalised and private grief 'with no heaving and gasping for breath'.

V

When the second part of the novel provides explicit insight into Sula's confused and contradictory psyche, the narrative most clearly seems to be presenting a black woman from perspectives which had hitherto not been articulated in African-American writing. Indeed one of the silences in such literature before 1970 was the sexual experience of black women as perceived by themselves. The reaction of the black men in Medallion to Sula is typical of how black people's sexuality has often been interpreted in literature in terms of male interests and desires. They cannot forgive Sula for having sex with white men even though black men lie with white women. Sula gives expression to her own sexuality in a way in which men have done so for generations; she seeks to satisfy herself not others and is willing to have sex without committing herself emotionally to her partners, discarding them as she wishes. This is an aspect of Sula to which Morrison herself has drawn attention in an interview:

> Sula is a masculine character in that sense. She will do the kinds of things normally only men do, that is why she is so strange. She really behaves like a man. She picks up a man, drops a man, the same way a man picks up a woman. And that's her thing. She's masculine in that sense. She's adventuresome, she trusts herself. She's not scared, she really ain't scared. And she is curious and will leave and try anything. (Harper and Stepto, 1979, 227)

Sula is subsequently labelled a 'bitch' because her promiscuity threatens the men's prowess and authority. The 'young men fantasise elaborate torture for her – just to get the saliva back in their mouths when they saw her' (112–13). Torture, like rape, has nothing to do with sex and everything to do with power, control and dominance. To some extent, the narrative's connection of the men's sexuality with their need to be dominant associates black men with those white men who rape black women in their fear of unfettered sexuality.

Significantly it is when Sula is most promiscuous that she is most obviously labelled as 'other'; her association with the plague of robins is consolidated in community lore and the allegation that she deliberately watched her mother burn to death acquires new credence: 'So they laid broomsticks across their doors at night and sprinkled salt on porch steps' (113). The challenge which she presents is underscored by the different ways in which her birthmark is read by observers; Nel's children see it as a 'scary black thing', which is how Sula herself is increasingly perceived by the community, while Jude, as we noted earlier, sees it as a rattlesnake. The ferocity of their labelling of Sula is an index of their fear of her unfettered sexuality. An increasing tension develops between the community's view of Sula which is alienating and alienated and the narrative's delineation of her sexuality which is increasingly intimate and encompassing. The focus upon her increasing desire to 'assert herself in the act' and the emphasis upon her 'post-coital privateness' give expression to areas of female sexual experience of which her partners are ignorant or to which they are indifferent: 'Whenever she introduced her private thoughts into their rubbings or goings, they hooded their eyes. They taught her nothing but love tricks, shared nothing but worry, gave nothing but money' (121). In the introduction to this book we referred to Koenen's (1985) argument that the grand-daughters of the black female-headed households, Sula in *Sula* and Hagar in *Song in Solomon*, evidenced 'generational degeneration' in their return to possessive love. But Koenen fails to distinguish between Sula and Hagar, whom we will discuss in the next chapter, and between the roles embraced by women for themselves and those imposed by patriarchy. The relationship between Sula and Ajax acquires significance within this framework. Ajax is not threatened by Sula as other men in the community appear to be. He is attractive to women because he makes them feel important; he listens to them and does not try to patronise or control them. In their lovemaking Sula is able to be, and enjoys being, on top. In the account of the lovemaking between them, the narrative gives expression to the intensity of sexual experience from the woman's point of view and the way in which she tries to control the orgasm so that it is right for her.

Sula, like *The Bluest Eye*, is not usefully approached through perceptions and reading habits derived from the European novel. The titular character in *Sula* is introduced late into the novel and 'killed off' before the end. The novel's centre is literally a blank and there are numerous ellipses and loose ends. In its emphasis on a relationship between two black women, delineated from a woman's perspective, and in the way in which it extends the African-American woman's need to create her own notion of selfhood to her need to have control over her own sexuality *Sula* breaks new ground. But in both these areas the novel is ambiguous for Sula herself, sharing characteristics with the traditional African trickster, challenges the community and in this point of focalisation causes readers to constantly reinterpret what they read. In particular there is a kaleidoscopic model of self and behaviour in the novel which confounds attempts to read it in terms of a binary structure or traditional, unified models of self.

4

Song of Solomon (1977)

I

As an African-American with a long-standing interest in deconstructing the white frame of reference by which black people have been defined, it is not surprising that in *Song of Solomon* Morrison should appropriate *the* archetype of white American literature: the romance narrative. But although *Song of Solomon* uses a traditional Euro-American mode of narrative, it would be misleading to interpret the novel only from this standpoint. The favoured ontology in the book is distinctly African, embracing black folktales and African legends and giving priority to African values.

Song of Solomon is based around the search of a young black man, Milkman Dead, for his legacy. He has been brought up in a family where his father has shunned his own community, whilst striving to become a small businessman respected by white people. His mother has been ostracised by her husband because he believed he had discovered her in a necrophiliac relationship with her father. Whilst Milkman's early adulthood passes in years of irresponsibility and indifference to the emerging civil rights struggles of the time, his quest for the lost family gold eventually becomes a search for spiritual values and the black ancestry in which he had previously shown no interest and which had been denied also by his father. His spiritual mentor in this search and the guardian of the lore he hopes to find is his aunt, Pilate, another member of the family disowned by his father because she is not respectable enough for him.

In the Preface to *The House of The Seven Gables* (1851), Nathaniel Hawthorne asserted that 'when a writer calls his work a Romance, it need hardly be observed that he wishes to claim a certain latitude, both as to its fashion and material, which he would not have felt himself entitled to assume had he professed to be writing a Novel'. A definition of romance, therefore, is difficult almost by definition. However, it is clear that for many nineteenth-century American writers the latitude which Hawthorne claimed for romance included working with folklore, myth and ritual; exploring anti-rational structures and levels of meaning; dramatising the instinctual and the passional. Quite apart from the Puritan and Calvinistic distrust of mimetic representation in the arts, it was inevitable perhaps that a form of writing which embraced the mythical, the instinctual and the anti-rational would acquire a special place, as Toni Morrison (1992) herself has argued, in nineteenth-century American culture.

In Morrison's view, romance as 'an exploration of anxiety imported from the shadows of European culture', enabled American writers to confront:

> Americans' fear of being outcast, of failing, of powerlessness; their fear of boundarylessness, of Nature unbridled and crouched for attack; their fear of the absence of so-called civilization; their fear of loneliness, of aggression both external and internal. (37)

Song of Solomon is a romance in both the nineteenth-century American sense and, as we shall discuss later, in the European sense. It has features in common with nineteenth-century American romance: it works with myth, folklore and ritual; and it involves anti-rational structures and levels of meaning. But many of the mythical and folklore elements come from Africa and the anti-rational elements, as we shall see later, arise from an African, and hence African-American, ontology. Krumholz (1993) has argued that there is evidence of the influence of two African epics, the Mwindo epic and the Kambili epic (563–7). Moreover, the novel is not concerned with the fears of white America; the fears are those of black America – of the dissolution of black culture and of the erosion of black sensibilities by the pursuit of white values. Myth, folklore and ritual are the essential means of reclaiming the black cultural heritage in opposition to the white construction of blackness.

White America's construction of blackness is, to a considerable extent, a response to the white fears which Morrison outlines. As she points out, one of the most important strategies by which white

Americans confronted those fears was the transference of 'internal conflicts' to black slaves, 'conveniently bound and violently silenced black bodies':

> What rose up out of collective needs to allay internal fears and to rationalize external exploitation was an American Africanism – a fabricated brew of darkness, otherness, alarm, and desire that is uniquely American. (38)

The impact of this 'fabricated brew of darkness, otherness, alarm' is well illustrated in one of the most famous white romances of the nineteenth century, Mark Twain's *The Adventures of Huckleberry Finn* (1884). Misunderstood quite often as the story of a boy's moral awakening or as a piece of escapist, freedom-of-the-river fantasy, its full complexity has also been missed by those who have seen it as a polemic against slavery or as an indictment of white society. The real subject of the book is European-America's fear of black America and the final part of the novel makes explicit the white fear of losing control. Mrs Hotchkiss's increasingly exaggerated estimate of the number of negroes involved in freeing Jim is an indicator of this, as is the whites' reaction in wanting to skin every negro in the place. The warning left on the door of the hut significantly hints at a larger issue than the freeing of one slave: 'Beware. Trouble is Brewing. Keep a sharp lookout'.

In *Song of Solomon*, the way in which white people project such fears on to blacks is evident in the murder of Till who is also a victim of white fears of the sexuality of the negro: as we explained in the introduction, he is alleged to have whistled after one white woman and is accused of sleeping with others. In the novel, the black men who adopt or seek to adopt white, middle-class values do so within a context of entrenched, white power in a society which is frightened of them and which eventually denies them. The novel unfolds against a backdrop which describes how Not Doctor Street arose as a name for Mains Avenue because the whites refused to sanction the black name of Doctor Street. Moreover black people tended to refer to the Mercy Hospital as Not Mercy Hospital (it was not until 1931 that the first pregnant black woman was allowed to give birth in a ward instead of on the steps) and when a black person, Reba, wins a prize as the half-millionth customer of Sears and Roebuck, it is not publicised (46).

From her reading of nineteenth-century American romance, Morrison argues that the subject 'on the "mind" of the literature of the United

States', as texts such as *The Adventures of Huckleberry Finn* demonstrate, was the 'highly problematic construction of the American as a new white man'. Within this context it is ironic, and maybe deliberately so, that in *Song of Solomon* Morrison produces a work which uses American romance conventions to explore the appropriation of white, middle-class American values by African-Americans.

II

Despite its traditional emphasis upon initiation, renunciation, atonement and release through ritual divestment, the experiment with the quest narrative in *Song of Solomon* through Milkman's search for his legacy is determined by its radical content. For example it is unclear at first that Milkman is the central character. In many respects he is an unlikely hero; for much of the novel he is uncommitted, unimaginative and draws inaccurate or inappropriate conclusions. But then this is a novel which expresses the limitations of any one view and which in its very structure suggests that to elevate any individual to the status of a hero or any one point of view to the level of myth is reductive.

Each voice in the novel appears to provide only its own fragmented version of the truth – the text literally dramatises the gap between telling and what is told. In fact the way in which the narrative appears to eschew chronological development and linear structure suggests that this fragmentariness is at the heart of the novel's worldview. But through the interplay between different viewpoints, concepts such as community, authority, commitment and individuality, for example, are subjected to scrutiny.

Song of Solomon, like all of Morrison's work, gives priority to ambivalence and discrepancy, eschewing the tendency of Western, Aristotelian philosophical tradition to give credence to single, unified meaning, confident in its modes of ordering and classification. The same story, as Genevieve Fabre argues, is picked up in different places, retold and expanded into further complexity (McKay, 1988, 108). For example, Milkman's father, Macon Dead, explains the tension between himself and Milkman's mother, Ruth, to Milkman, alleging that Ruth had an unhealthy fixation for her father and he for her which culminated in Macon finding Ruth in bed with her deceased father, 'naked as a yard dog, kissing him' with his fingers in her mouth (73). Ruth's own version portrays herself as a lonely person who needed the support of her father: 'It was important for me to be in his presence, among his things, the things he used, had touched. Later it was important for me to know that he was in the world' (124). She accuses Macon of trying to kill Milkman and of killing her father by removing his medicine. Ruth now appears starved of affection by her father who was more interested in winning the respect of white people and acquiring a big house than in loving her as a father should. As a woman, she is driven to take her dead father as a clandestine lover, lying at his feet in the cemetery, because her husband has refused to make love to her in the twenty years they have been married. Each retelling of a story in the novel, as here, raises new questions suggesting that any one version of anything inevitably generates fresh interpretations.

As we shall see, *Song of Solomon* is a dialogical novel, a hybrid of multiple motifs and allusions. Medieval romance motifs are combined, for example, with biblical references and classical allusions. Black folklore, realism and the supernatural are woven together and in the Circe episode realism seems to collapse altogether beneath the weight of fabulation.

The priority which the novel gives to Milkman's journey should be placed, then, within the larger, fragmentary nature of the narrative as a whole. The numerous discourses which surround his journey have more importance in the novel than in the traditional romantic quest, accounting for the fact that it is some way into the novel before Milkman emerges as the central character. It is not simply a matter of Milkman's journey dominating the second half of the novel and the first half of the novel serving to provide a preparation for the hero's quest as Lee (1982) argues. Milkman emerges as the hero of the narrative at the same time as a hierarchy of values begins to emerge from the competing discourses of its first part.

Much of our understanding of Milkman's journey is teleological. The journey is from the North dominated by urban, white middle-class values to the black South and it is the latter which reveals the former fully for what it is. Milkman travels by plane, by bus and then by foot – emblematic of the way in which he sheds layers of his former cultural identity. The journey to Circe's home, the house of the servant who saved Pilate and Macon after their father was killed and who bears the name of Odysseus's guide to the lower world, is made difficult as much by his city clothes as by his ineptitude. Gradually, he loses his clothes, watch, suitcase and shoes, symbolising the white cultural values he has absorbed and assimilated at the expense of black values. The loss of the watch is especially significant because Milkman loses the Western concept of time which is essentially linear as opposed to a traditional African concept of time which is cyclical.

There is an additional element to all of this: the various competing discourses of the first part of the novel are within Milkman himself. His quest resolves the conflicts between North and South, male and female, white and black within his own psyche. In doing so, certain discourses which have been silenced emerge and become dominant in his spiritual-physical makeup.

The white peacock encountered by Milkman and Guitar as they seek to steal Pilate's gold suggests, as Lee (1982) points out, that in order to fly, the black person must reject the imposed white sociocultural baggage. White peacocks are usually only found in captivity, implying that the white cultural tradition is itself a captivity. Milkman admires the peacock's strut – epitomising how those blacks who imitate whites and assume white cultural values, such as Macon Dead in his Packard car and Ruth's father, acquire a similar kind of social strut. Ironically, Milkman realises that the peacock can fly no better than a chicken. Guitar's response encapsulates the problem:

> 'Too much tail', Guitar replies. 'All that jewelry weighs it down. Like vanity. Can't nobody fly with all that shit. Wanna fly, you got to give up the shit that weighs you down.' (179).

Hagar learns a similar lesson the hard way in repeating Pecola's mistake in *The Bluest Eye*. She comes to believe that voguish clothing and cosmetics will lift her skyward, but in the rain they literally fall to the streets. Giving up 'the shit that weighs you down', as Guitar puts it, involves considerable personal growth, self-awareness and personal pain. Hagar, like Milkman who was overnourished on breast milk, is a victim of obsessive love; she has not been able to develop sufficient inner strength and resilience. In this respect, the disintegration of her cosmetics in the rain symbolises the fragility of her own personality.

After the hunt in the South, Milkman acquires knowledge of himself, the community and Guitar. The decision to eat the heart of the slain bobcat, as Lee (1982) demonstrates, is redolent of the traditional ritual by which hunters internalised the courage of the prey. The description of the way in which the heart comes from the body 'as easily as yolk slips out of its shell' (282) reminds us of Guitar's point that Milkman is a shell which has to be broken.

This narrative of escape from the Dead household – dead in the spiritual sense as well as in name – is a story of growth reinforced by the interjection of the account of Corinthians, Milkman's sister. In becoming the 'amanuensis' of Michigan's Poet Laureate, Corinthians becomes an ornament within the elegant emptiness of a home where there is no passion. In this respect, Henry Porter's verse, with which he seeks to woo her, is an improvement upon the celebrated poetry. The relationship which Corinthians establishes with him moves from one based on hatred because of the shame she felt, to one in which she becomes a 'grown-up woman'.

III

The ways in which *Song of Solomon* gives more priority to the competing discourses within it than to Milkman's journey as such, which is where Lee (1982) places the emphasis, reflects its African-American concerns. The hero of the traditional quest is usually the child of distinguished parents. Milkman's ancestors are distinguished but in non-traditional ways; his own father, Macon Dead, Jnr, is a grotesque fairytale character whose lust for gold has made him one of the most affluent and most hated black property owners. However, his name epitomises how much his fixation with white-defined respectability has cost him in personal, social and spiritual terms even though his accumulation of wealth is part of his attempt to overcome oppression, prejudice, poverty and lack of a formal education. It is Guitar who makes explicit the connection between the imposed name, Dead, the appropriation of white values and a more generalised and pervasive white control: 'White men want us dead or quiet – which is the same thing as dead . . . They want us, you know, "universal", human, "no race consciousness" ' (222). This is further embodied in the car Macon drives with a winged woman on its bonnet, 'riding backward like flying blind', and in the way in which the black community calls the vehicle 'Macon Dead's hearse'. The counterpoint to the figure on the bonnet of the car is the way in which Corinthians spreadeagles herself across Porter's antiquated vehicle; flying to save herself. Significantly the first trial which Milkman has to undergo in the South in the second half of the novel, a fight in a general store in Shalimar, Virginia, is started because the local people are offended by his money and sense of privilege: 'They looked at his skin and saw it was black as theirs, but they knew he had the heart of the white men who came to pick them up in the trucks when they needed anonymous, faceless laborers' (266). The importance of this motif within the novel is underscored by Macon's ironic naming of his daughter, First Corinthians, since it is in St Paul's First Epistle to the Corinthians that personal pride, vanity and ambition are attacked.

In the traditional quest, the hero takes revenge on his father and achieves rank and honours. Milkman, in a process which begins when he strikes his father, eventually frees himself from his father's obsessive capitalism and discovers that he is a descendant of Solomon Sugarman, a progenitor of 21 children, renowned for his ability to fly – commemorated in a nursery rhyme and the naming of his launching site, Solomon's Leap. Here the novel does not simply parody the European quest narrative, it also draws on the African concept of the mythological hero and betrays the importance which African culture traditionally attaches to the ancestor. In 'Rootedness: the Ancestor as Foundation', Morrison describes ancestors as a 'sort of timeless people whose relationships to the characters are benevolent, instructive, and protective, and they provide a certain kind of wisdom' (Morrison in Evans, 1984, 343). The title *Song of Solomon* suggests the biblical song of ancestral wisdom and from the beginning the novel is presided over by the figure of Milkman's forefather. Indeed, it has the epigraph: 'The fathers may soar/And the children may know their names'. As Segy (1976) argues:

> The mythological hero who represented special valor because of his exceptional services to the tribe in the legendary past was regarded as a model, the embodiment of the best of human potentiality. As descendants of his hero, the living through identification with him derived a special tribal pride which was the basis for their ethnocentrism. (8)

Song of Solomon is framed by the African-American vernacular tradition of the flying African. The song which Pilate sings to accompany Milkman's birth is a variant of this Gullah folktale of the ancestor who flew back to Africa to escape the trap of slavery and Milkman's leap at the end of the novel aligns him with Solomon. The importance of this kind of identification with ancestors in African culture is again stressed by Segy (1976):

> He experienced being part of the mythical past. He was able to identify himself with that which was presented to him as permanent

and sacred reality. Because of this identification he was able to step out of his ordinary, egocentred daily life. His individual life was depersonalized, elevated. (8)

However, even this concept of sacred reality represented by the ancestor is open in this particular instance to different lines of interpretation. In abandoning Ryna, Solomon is identified with a number of male characters in the book who abandon women, including Jake Solomon, Macon Dead and Milkman himself. Here, as de Weever (1991) points out, the text expounds the potentially dangerous routes out of life, away from the need for commitment and stability, implicit in the Greek myths of Icarus and Daedalus and the folktales of the flying African (28–9).

The novel also develops the traditional focus upon ancestry in African culture in an African-American context through its emphasis on the significance of naming. The reclamation of true identity is crucial to black people who in slavery were named by others. As Guitar explains to Milkman: 'Niggers get their names the way they get everything else – the best way they can' (88). Ironically, a drunken Union army officer working for the Freedman's Bureau put the name of Macon's father's birth place and the fact that his father was dead in the wrong place on the registration form. The fact that Macon, Jr, has inherited this false name highlights the way in which he is a grotesque distortion of his father. His father's real name was Jake, but his son is more like his biblical namesake, crafty and patriarchal. For Jake, property was not mere property, but the symbol of a bond between the land and the community. The man who appears to Macon, Jr, after his father has been killed by the white Butlers reminds him of his father – indeed he might be the father's ghost. In fact, he is the ghostly distortion of Jake which Macon is to become. The old white man hoarding the gold in the cave to which the apparition takes Macon is an adaptation of a stock situation from the traditional quest, gold being hidden in an ogre's cave. Although it cannot be interpreted solely in this light, the borrowed motif draws attention to itself: offering a parody of the whiteness which Macon is to assume.

Of course Milkman's own nickname has ignominious origins; because his mother breastfed him for much longer than normal it was given to him by Freddie, the janitor, who likes to believe he is a friend of the family. The name serves to exacerbate the tension between Milkman and his father. Although Macon doesn't understand the origins of the name he recognises that it sounds 'dirty, intimate, and hot' thereby reminding him of his wife's abnormal fixation for her father and the passion which he denies in himself and in his children. His son's name compounds the shame of his own name:

> Surely, he thought, he and his sister had some ancestor, some lithe young man with onyx skin and legs as straight as cane stalks, who had a name that was real. A name given to him at birth with love and seriousness. A name that was not a joke, nor a disguise, nor a brand name. (17–18)

In the traditional European quest either during or before pregnancy there is usually an omen against the birth which seems to endanger the father. Milkman is compared before he is born to a little bird (9) and he is the first child born in Mercy Hospital. His birth accompanied by Pilate's Song of Sugarman is also marked by the insurance salesman's leap from the top of the hospital. But once again it is important not to see the circumstances of Milkman's birth only as an appropriation of a European literary convention. The circumstances around Milkman's birth serve to emphasise key myths. The myth of the flying African is appropriated as is the sacredness of the ancestor. Singing is an essential part of the Gospel church and Pilate's 'powerful contralto' suggests that the events which are occurring are in some way sacred. The song proves to be a significant clue in Milkman's identification of his forefather.

IV

In the European romance narrative, the main geographical element is provided by the lands through which the hero travels on his quest. However, *Song of Solomon* presents us with an ideological geography, as it were. There are three overlapping zones in which people live and which have been created by the white political system. As Guitar tries to explain to Milkman:

> 'No Geography? Okay, no geography. What about some history in your tea? Or some sociopolitico – No. That's still geography. Goddam, Milk, I do believe my whole life's geography.' (114)

The three zones as portrayed in the novel reinterpret the geography of the USA in terms of a sociopolitical dialectic: a black centre which is also a disenfranchised community, a zone which is a white zone, and a zone between them which allows for entry into the white zone but to a limited degree only. Indeed, the sociospace occupied by Macon Dead is the overlap between the white and black zones. It is a no-person's land as exemplified in his walk down Fifteenth Street:

> Scattered here and there, his houses stretched up beyond him like squat houses with hooded eyes . . . now they did not seem to belong to him at all – in fact he felt as though the houses were in league with one another to make him feel like the outsider, the propertyless, landless wanderer. (27)

By contrast Milkman's entry to the community occurs in the black heart of the South in the fight in the general store provoked by the way in which Milkman has black skin but 'the heart of the white men who came to pick them up in the trucks when they needed anonymous, faceless laborers' (266). The zones are fluid, of course; political pressures from within can change them as can individual heroes. This is what Guitar, through violence, purports to do even though he operates in the tradition of the trickster and other ambivalent, archetypal figures who, by challenging the hero, push him toward his destination.

The legacy which Macon hopes his son will inherit is the one built by power and property in order to move the boundaries so that the family will one day become integrated with white society. In Europe, social status has been traditionally assessed in terms of land which, passed on through generations, signifies power and elitism. White America's puritan heritage gave the nation a sense of election through predestination, an ethic which confirmed the importance of the individual in building the nation's economic prosperity. In America, property and money translated as success through work became an index of a person's spiritual and moral value. In the nation's ideology, wealth was not associated with greed or exploitation but with the exploitation of inner personal resources. Material poverty became an indicator not of a social problem, but of individual spiritual poverty. The effect of this ideology on Macon Dead is evident in the way in which he is ashamed of Pilate, fearing that the white men in the bank on whose support he is dependent and whose respect he seeks may discover that she is his sister.

We are never told exactly why Robert Smith fails to fly at the beginning of the novel, but we suspect that it is because he is too far removed from his heritage, which is also Macon Dead's failing. For some time, Macon believes that gold will set him free. Milkman repeats this mistake and when he enters the cave to find the gold his father has told him about there is a significant absence of light.

If we overstress the elements of the European romance narrative in this novel we might overlook the African myths which also determine the structure. Macon Dead, Jr, is a version of a character, Anaanu, from a very old West African folktale which found its way into America as Brer Rabbit and which is the basis of *Tar Baby* (1981). In one version of the original story, for example, Anaanu is a trickster spider who escapes famine by faking death and at night eats his fill. Macon, like Anaanu, chooses dispossession in order to achieve material gain. Anaanu's pretence at being dead is a form of disguise and Macon, too, in his denial of his sister, Pilate, and his family adopts a pretence. Both Anaanu and Macon give up their place within the community for personal gain. Morrison develops this West African folktale within a particular American context and within the frame of the Euro-American quest story.

The European romantic quest has been readily employed in white American literature to explore ways in which the American dream of spiritual greatness became a dream of material greatness. Whilst this transformation has been treated with considerable bitterness in some white American texts, others which employ the quest motif, such as F. Scott Fitzgerald's *The Great Gatsby*, stop short of condemning the desire for wealth even though they expose the corrupting influence of it in particular examples. Gatsby himself epitomises the American ideal of the self-made man and the capacity in America for people to make their own identities. In becoming Jay Gatsby, James Gatz escapes from his own origins and his naïve quest is linked to Arthurian legendary heroes such as Sir Galahad and Sir Percival and the quest for the Holy Grail. The grail which is Gatsby's quest is a romantic notion of perfect femininity – eventually exposed as false – based on the outward appearance of a corrupt and degenerate system. Gatsby's creation of himself and his quest are compared in the novel to frontier versions of the concept of the self-made man – as a boy, Gatsby made notes on self-improvement on a fly leaf of a copy of *Hopalong Cassidy* and his career begins when he meets Dan Cody, a relic of an earlier America – in order to demonstrate the corruption of the original dream.

In *Song of Solomon*, Morrison combines a number of mythologies so that each acts as a critique of the others. Up to a point, Macon Dead epitomises the white American concept of the self-made man, but, unlike Gatsby, he did not choose his own name. Unlike Gatsby, Macon Dead, Jr, comes to experience a rejecting society and the past which is corrupted in his quest is not a white heritage. In *The Great Gatsby* the dream can only be achieved by overturning any larger sense of moral responsibility for others. In Morrison's novel, although Macon Dead, too, can only realise his quest by eschewing any moral responsibility for others, he also rejects his black cultural heritage:

> Macon Dead dug in his pocket for his keys, and curled his fingers around them, letting their bunchy solidity calm him. They were the keys to all the doors of his houses (only four true houses; the rest were really shacks), and he fondled them from time to time as he walked down Not Doctor Street to his office. At least he thought of it as his office, had even painted the word OFFICE on the door. But the plate-glass window contradicted him. In peeling gold letters arranged in a semicircle, his business establishment was declared to be Sonny's Shop. (17)

The fact that his office is situated on Not Doctor Street compounds the irony in this passage because the name is a symbol of black resistance. The name of the previous black occupant of the premises reminds Macon and the reader of the past which he can never finally eradicate. The previous name suggests that the shop was at the centre of the community whereas Macon's use of the premises as an office for his property business implies a greater emphasis on the pursuit of individual wealth and success at the expense of community.

The tension between Macon's and Ruth's aspirations for their son is part of a larger discourse within *Song of Solomon* around internal difference in the black community. Macon has little regard for university education and Ruth's aspirations for her son to enter university focus on the status which the medical degree will bring her as well as him, epitomised in the silver-backed brushes engraved with his initials, the abbreviated designation of doctor. The coincidence here again suggests how Milkman, like many black people, is not in control of his own destiny and this is bound up in the fact that he has been unable to choose his own name. The novel suggests on many levels that whereas black people become part of the American middle class they do not have the same licence as Gatsby, for example, to create their own identities which is the ideology on which the American middle-class pursuit of prosperity is founded. Thrown into confusion concerning his identity, Milkman's examination of his face before the mirror, his firm jawline and splendid teeth, reminds us significantly of the way in which slaves were examined in the marketplace and of a history with which black people still have to struggle (69).

V

Milkman's true inheritance, black cultural identity and ancestry, is provided by the women and particularly his aunt, Pilate. Although the epigraph mentions only the forefathers in the novel and the book is dedicated to 'Daddy', Morrison creates a space in which the women may be recognised and may assume importance. In many respects, the women are locked out of the soulless, material-orientated, patriarchal world in which the men – Macon Dead and Dr Foster – are locked. Pilate – 'Christ Killing Pilate' – has the worst possible name as Fabre points out (McKay, 1988, 109). Yet she understands the power of naming; the only name her father wrote hangs in a little box from her ear. She becomes quite literally Milkman's pilot or guiding force. She challenges his indifference and initiates him into the legacy of which black womankind are the guardians, a legacy of wisdom and beliefs. Pilate's lack of a navel associates her with Eve, source of innocence and, paradoxically, of primal knowledge.

 Pilate's perfect, soft-boiled eggs symbolise a balance of which Macon and herself seem separated spheres. Whilst Macon appears to follow and exaggerate the side of Jake which wants to own property and which values the status so accrued, Pilate embodies the spiritual and community-orientated part of him. Pilate's own home contrasts significantly with Macon's. Ruth and her daughter make fake roses and the only confirmation Ruth can find of her existence is the ugly spreading watermark left on the dining-room table from a bowl which once held fresh flowers. When Lena eventually wakes to what is happening to her, the outburst recalls Guitar's condemnation of how white people want black people quiet and 'dead': 'I was the one who started making artificial roses . . . I loved to do it. It kept me . . . quiet. That's why they make those people in the asylum weave baskets and make rag rugs. It keeps them quiet. If they didn't have the baskets they might find out what's really wrong and . . . do something. Something terrible' (213). Her hesitation before she can bring herself to say the word 'quiet' underscores its significance, for her and for her whole family, as well as the pain in the realisation. The phrase 'something terrible' is set apart and as such highlights the fear whites have of blacks who rise against their confinement. In the description of the suicidal leap at the outset of the novel, roses occur along with wings and song as specific images, each of which eventually provides this multi-layered text with a sense of coherence around the subjects of freedom, spirituality, life-in-death, the value of myth and the role of the ancestor: 'The sight of Mr Smith and his wide blue wings transfixed them for a few seconds, as did the woman's singing and the roses strewn about' (6).

Pilate's house is filled with the smell of nature with which she is associated, of the forest and of blackberries. Of course her association with nature is another indicator of how she has taken after the positive side of Jake's character, reminding us of the love he had for his peach trees and his ability to make his crops increase and multiply. When Lena turns her anger against Milkman for the way he has ignored them she draws attention to the dying maple tree (122). Significantly Morrison herself has pointed out, in Jaye and Watts (1981), that none of Gatsby's people achieves a fulfilling life in the natural environment, suggesting the importance which she attaches to this aspect of her characters such as Pilate (36).

However, as we suggested earlier, this is a complicated novel not easily reducible to binary opposites. Pilate is a character in the novel of whom we can also be critical. Her rootlessness is symbolised by the rocks which she carries, each one a remembrance of a place to which she has been and, like the name she carries in a box and her bag of bones, they symbolise her search for a place of belonging. Some critics have emphasised not her symbolic strengths but her general passivity, and indeed the passivity of most of the female characters compared with the male characters, and have seen this as confirming the male bias in the epigraph to the novel.

It would be wrong to see Pilate, as some critics have, as a totally negative character for such an interpretation would ignore the way in which the women are seen as the guardians of worthwhile knowledge which the men have to acquire. As Nancy Walker (1986) has pointed out, the white romance in America usually embodied a dream of escape that is both peculiarly American and identifiably masculine. Historically, the political and physical experiences of settling and exploring a wilderness required powers that have commonly been granted to men rather than women. However *Song of Solomon* casts women in a better light than the men: Macon Dead, Ruth's father and Milkman himself are selfish, uncaring people. Macon Dead is ruthless with delinquent tenants, wants to own people and worships wealth. Ruth's father is seen as a 'miracle doctor' by whites, but, obsessed with caste, he does little for blacks. Milkman deserts Hagar and most of the men violate family bonds.

VI

At the heart of the reclamation of a non-Western worldview in *Song of Solomon* is a concern with a preconscious mode of awareness encapsulated in myth. Of course myth may be perceived in mythologising cultures as a means of preserving the wisdom of precedents based on ancestral laws – precedents which often connect ancestral pasts with cosmogonic events. The title of the novel itself reminds us of Solomon's song of ancestral wisdom. But myth may also be preserved as the poetic verbalisation of the unconscious and preconscious. In fact *Song of Solomon* offers a complex model of the unconscious which is close to that which Segy claims is characteristic of mythologising cultures. Pilate and Macon would seem to represent the separating out of the two spheres of the unconscious which Segy identifies. Pilate's own sensibility and creative existence give expression to an inner truth derived from her grasp of a supreme reality beyond her everyday existence, a sense of the wholeness of the order of things. She appears motivated by what Segy would refer to as her 'ontological natural self', a psychological self as it exists before the conditioning of the environment. Macon and Milkman are motivated by an unconscious which has been shaped by the circumstances of their lives and the 'pre-reflective awareness' which Pilate appears to possess has been falsified by interpretation, as is demonstrated by Milkman's repeated failure to ask the right questions. In the book reclaiming the black legacy involves reclaiming a mythological and pre-reflective awareness and all this might appear simply romantic. Distrust of logical thought and empirical rationalism emerged in America in the 1950s and 1960s as part of a counter-establishment culture which led many white American writers to experiment with hallucinogenic drugs and philosophies in search of alternatives to Euro-American models of conceptualising the world. Yet this recurring preoccupation among certain American writers of the 1950s and 1960s was underpinned by perceived differences between Western and non-Western worldviews summarised by Segy (1976):

It is possible to trace present-day Western civilization to Socratic, Platonic, and Aristotelian concepts predicated upon man's intellect, his logical thought processes, which evolved into a pragmatic, scientific, materialistic outlook. The African cultures followed another path similar to the spiritual teachings of the Hebrew prophets, Buddha, Lao Tzu, or Jesus, and produced another way of life based upon man's spiritual needs, a socio-religious, well-ordered, communal (and not individualistic) integrated way of life. (17)

Song of Solomon is different in its concern with states of consciousness from the eclecticism of white American literature of the 1950s and 1960s which fused early nineteenth-century European romantic thought with non-Western philosophy. Morrison's novel is concerned with reclaiming and not simply discovering the priorities of a culture founded upon different philosophical and spiritual principles from those of the West. As Wilentz (1992) argues, African values are privileged in the novel, as exemplified by Pilate who illustrates the role of the African female ancestor in transmitting familial and cultural knowledge; she makes the potion to improve Macon and Ruth's sex life (86). Indeed, Milkman's acceptance of myth and the supernatural stems from his acceptance that Pilate is without a navel, and it is this openness, though it takes him 20 years to act on it, which separates him, as Wilentz says, from his father.

Song of Solomon has a moral self-confidence which is not to be found in many contemporary white American novels. Bigsby (1980) has gone so far as to see the post-Second World War black writer as the exponent of a liberalism which the white American novel has rejected. This moral self-confidence derives from the belief that there are available truths concealed beneath illusion and falsehood and, as Bigsby claims, this is surely a liberal presumption. But Bigsby fails to locate the source of the narrative's assertion that there are truths to be realised in the reclamation of the priorities of a non-Western culture. His thesis seems to shoehorn the novel into a white liberal tradition to which it simply does not belong:

And, in terms of black writing, self-perception frequently comes to the protagonist in a visit to the underworld, in a mock death, a dive down into the underground of self and society alike . . . (162)

What Bigsby says here is clearly applicable to *Song of Solomon*, but he does not recognise the romance formula in his own survey of black fiction and, more seriously, how the black novel subverts the romance genre. Bigsby discusses the black protagonist in terms of alienation and estrangement more appropriate to the way in which protagonists in novels by white writers felt cast adrift on the irrepressible new:

This is perhaps why so many black novels are set in that past which is part tangible and part mythic; a usable past which can be turned to the purpose of locating a self which had been cut adrift in an American environment it could not define and whose direction it could not deflect. It is a past, too, which must be set against that projected by white historians . . . For the black writer, as for the Jew, the past is to be claimed, the implications of an alienated self to be denied, a tradition of moral responsibility to be accepted. (157)

Despite the good points which are made here, Bigsby's use of 'claimed' rather than 'reclaimed' is significant. For there is insufficient recognition that we are dealing with more than just a past. The novel is concerned with the mythologising nature of black as opposed to white culture and of the differences between black and white concepts of moral responsibility.

Nevertheless, Bigsby is right to assert that there is something refreshing about the strength of the moral assuredness of African-American fiction after the emphasis of the non-liberal white novel upon 'cosmic conspiracies, fragmented layers of experience whose coherences are contingent, a self which is either a distorting mirror or a transparent membrane offering a pathway to ultimate nirvana . . .' (154). Certainly, *Song of Solomon* does not present the nihilistic vision of many postmodern works that behind every construction of so-called truth lies only another construction. Nor does it abandon the notion that individual projects are worthwhile for the individual and the community simply because all human projects are constructed and inevitably limited although it does submit them to scrutiny. Macon Dead's project, for example, is obviously very limited. So too in a different way is Guitar's involvement with the Seven Days. Guitar, like

Milkman, wants Pilate's gold. But, like Milkman before he realises his true legacy, Guitar's project courts death even though the name ironically echoes creation in the Book of Genesis. Arguing for a programme of indiscriminate retaliatory murder of whites in revenge for the murder of blacks, Guitar can love black people in the aggregate, but he cannot love individuals nor give sufficient weight to individual responsibility. Bent on revenge in the name of love, he is divided against himself rather like his father, sawn in two parts at the saw mill.

The concept of individual moral responsibility in this novel is not the same as that to be found in white American liberal novels. The moral vision underpinning the narrative fuses recognition of the black cultural legacy and the reclamation of its priorities, including a community-orientated sense of responsibility, with a reclamation of a mythological cultural framework. In order to fly Milkman has to recognise the importance of his cultural legacy and acquire a commitment towards the wider black community. In the early part of the novel Milkman tries to avoid commitment. Indeed, his name suggests infancy and the egocentricity of a young child from which Milkman has to develop. Overnourished by his mother's milk, he fails to grow until the interjection of Lena's accusation that he has victimised others with his egotism. Within this context, Pilate's explanation as to why she has kept the bag of bones with her makes Milkman ashamed that he has betrayed his mentor who presided over the 'miracle' of his birth. His relationship with Sweet in the South is an indicator of his growth: he is able to enter a reciprocal relationship which culminates in a joyous swim in a spring, symbolising baptism and rebirth.

The black cultural heart of the South is a mythic and perhaps finally an unconvincing counterpoint to the North. The superiority of the men in the South is indicated, as Lee (1982) has explained, by their names, the names of poets, kings and men of God: Omar, King Walker, Luther, Solomon, Calvin Breakstone. They possess a 'pre-reflection awareness' of the kind embodied by Pilate. Milkman observes incredulously that the men and their hunting dogs speak to each other in:

> . . . it was what was there before language . . . And if they could talk to animals, and the animals could talk to them, what didn't they know about human beings? Or the earth itself, for that matter. (278)

The importance of belief over fact (the world of science) is evidenced in the sack of bones which Pilate carries. In the end it does not matter whether the bones are of her husband (as she tells the police) or of a murdered white man (as she believes) or of her father (as Milkman informs her). The bones are a symbol of an obligation to a past event and to a relationship.

Song of Solomon then is a novel which, although it appropriates the characteristics of the European romance formula, cannot be seen only in those terms. It is a dialogical novel in which the same incident or character is seen from different viewpoints and in which competing discourses are highlighted. Although concepts such as community, commitment, authority and individuality are thereby subjected to scrutiny, a hierarchy of favoured positions emerges in the course of the text which have their origins in African-American culture. Over-emphasising how the novel appears to provide an ironic version of the European quest might lead the reader to underestimate how its experiment with the romantic quest form is determined by black concerns, African myth and aspects of an African ontology.

5

Tar Baby (1981)

I

Tar Baby is concerned with the relationship which develops between Jadine, a light-skinned African-American woman raised in the Caribbean by her aunt, Ondine, and her husband, who are servants of a retired white factory owner, and Son, a dark-skinned fugitive on the run for murdering his wife. Brought up and educated at the University of the Sorbonne on the money of her aunt's employer, Jadine leads a life which revolves around New York and Paris where she has become an art historian and a model. Ostensibly we might think that Jadine is the tar baby of the title; however the novel is more complex than this and the label seems applicable to different characters at different points in the narrative.

Like Morrison's first novel, *The Bluest Eye*, *Tar Baby* is concerned with what Eleanor Traylor calls 'the carcinogenic disease eating away at the ancestral spirit of the race' (McKay, 1988, 146). It, too, focuses upon African-Americans who shun their black identities in favour of the values and norms of white America, for example, Sydney and Ondine, the black servants of the white retired factory owner, Valerian Street, and their niece, Jadine. Both servants, as Mbalia (1991) observes, obviously 'identify more with their employers and their employers' culture than they do with their own people and their own culture' (71), evidenced in the way in which they allow Valerian's wife, Margaret, to call them Kingfish and Beuleh rather than by their real names and in the way in which Ondine refers to Margaret's kitchen as her own. The origins of their position lie in the Old South which encouraged an alliance between the white upper classes and the slave elite who still sought respect from the white man on the white man's terms long after the American Civil War had ended.

The novel, however, like *The Bluest Eye*, is as much concerned with the ideological nature of language as with the way in which individual African-Americans have been seduced by white values. This is evident when Sydney proclaims his origins as 'one of those industrious Philadelphian negroes' to Son, the black fugitive who has entered Valerian's home: 'I am a Phil-a-delphia Negro mentioned in the book of the very same name. My people owned drugstores and taught school while yours [Son's] were still cutting their faces open so as to be able to tell one of you from the other' (164). Sydney's reiteration of European contempt for African culture, compared with the way in which the woman-in-yellow in the novel proudly bears two upside-down V's scored into each of her cheeks, is an attempt to accord himself more status. It calls into question the meanings attached to the word 'civilised' which is not actually used by Sydney but implied throughout. 'Civilisation' is a concept which cannot be evoked without qualification especially when differing European and African perspectives are called into play. In fact Sydney here exploits the potential of language to carry a multiplicity of meanings, both explicit and implicit, from his self-conscious pronunciation of the world 'Phil-a-delphia' to the way superiority is attached to written culture through the emphasis on the word 'book', to his derogatory description of the ethnic traditions of facial adornment. Throughout *Tar Baby*, possession of European prejudices about blacks is an important indicator of the extent to which individuals have lost contact with their roots. Jadine's reflection on the way Son unsettles her is riddled with stereotypical assumptions. She has become so far removed from black people that she has come to believe that they are either 'creeps' or possessed of rare sexual energy and dynamism (126).

The narrative structure of *The Bluest Eye*, as we have seen, is focused around the disparity between the different meanings which American English carries for African-Americans compared with white middle-class Americans. The novel explores the extent to which African-Americans are caught up not only in an alien ideology but in an alienating language. Henry Louis Gates, Jr (1992) argues that this is a central fact for the black person in America. In order to illustrate the point in an essay 'Writing, "Race", and the Difference it Makes', he cites the story of Edmund Laforest, a prominent member of the Haitian literary movement, who committed suicide by jumping from a bridge with a Larousse dictionary tied around his neck. Since the ability to use language has traditionally been the litmus-test of civilisation, African-

Americans have had to establish themselves within European post-Enlightenment civilisation through the language of their oppressors even while drawing on an African ontology or an African mythopeaia. In *Tar Baby*, these twin complexities are further explored within a tripartite focus, connecting meaning, race and difference.

Although *Tar Baby*, unlike the other novels, does not directly cover a broad period of time – it is set exclusively in the period from autumn 1979 to autumn 1980 – it incorporates a wide range of perspectives through its use of myths and concepts whose meanings have undergone change in different periods and cultural contexts. In this respect it utilises a characteristic of language which the twentieth-century Russian critic, Mikhail Bakhtin, made the focus of much of his work: that language is not a unified, fixed or stable system, but as a social and historical process it is always in a state of flux. The initial description of Valerian's lifestyle indicates the novel's interest in this theme for he reads only the mail, having given up books because 'the language in them had changed so much – stained with rivulets of disorder and meaninglessness' (12). One of the central concerns of *Tar Baby* is the way in which meaning itself is very difficult to pin down, being plural and contested rather than singular and uncontested. Indeed when Valerian tells his niece to read *The Little Prince*, he emphasises 'pay attention not to what it says, but what it means' (71).

The exact meaning of language is elusive for many reasons, another of which is also fundamental to *Tar Baby*. Meaning, subject to what the French theorist, Derrida, identifies as 'the "active", moving discord of different forces', is endlessly deferred because it is always relational, never self-present or self-constituted (1982, 18). This phenomenon Derrida labelled *différance*, a word which conflates the senses of difference and deferment. For example, if we consider the word 'family' which recurs in the first novel, we see it has come to represent, or signify, a particular type of group of people related to each other in some way. In the dictionary, the word is said to have a range of possible meanings such as: members of a household; the descendants of a common ancestor; a group of persons or nations united by political or religious ties; a group of allied genera; or a subdivision of an order. These associations are arbitrary, there is nothing in the word, for example, which suggests a household of related people living together; we have learned to associate the two aspects through custom and convention. But the word is also part of a larger system of language; the signifier 'family' gives us the concept of 'family', or signified of 'family', because it is different from a lot of other signifiers such as 'commune' or 'household'. Thus meaning arises from the interplay of an infinite number of signifiers and as much from what a signifier is *not* as what it is. For this reason, Gideon, one of the black servants, has difficulty explaining the words 'blood bank' and 'eye bank' to his wife, Thérèse. The word 'bank' confuses the issue for her, suggesting that American doctors take organs in order to sell them to rich people. Thérèse is unable to understand the relational nature of language and, indeed, the focus of much of *Tar Baby* is on the ways in which meanings are endlessly deferred, rather like Margaret's son in the novel, always promising to turn up but never finally arriving. The French theorist, Derrida, identified what he called 'switch points' in language, linguistic levers which ensure that words, again like Margaret's son, never reach their final destinations because they are intercepted, detoured and relayed (1987, 78). It is appropriate that a novel by a black writer, especially a black woman writer, should concern itself with the way in which meaning arises from an interplay of signifiers and is endlessly deferred. Homi Bhabha (1994) points out the stereotype is not simply a misrepresentation of reality. The colonial subject is denied 'access to the recognition of difference' and to that 'possibility of difference and circulation which would liberate the signifier of *skin/culture* from the fixations of racial typology' (75). In other words, the skin colour, hair and ultimately race of African-Americans become 'ineradicable signs' of negative difference, unable to break free of this fixity.

II

One of the sets of meanings which appear to be endlessly deferred, demonstrating how meaning never stays the same from context to context, are those clustered around the concept of the tar baby story itself. As Werner observes: 'Assuming new meanings as its context shifts . . . each new version of the myth influences the consciousness of the individuals who, even though they accept the myths that they inherit, gradually assign them new meanings as signs that can be transformed into further myths' (McKay, 1988, 154–5). But before pursuing the implications of how the meanings of the tar baby myth have been altered by the various chains of signifiers in which it has become entangled, we need to return to a question which we asked in the previous chapter: why should Morrison draw on myth? At one level myth is a metaphor for human experience, a means of communicating that experience and of ascertaining its meaning. de Weever (1991) sees the reclamation of myth by African-American writers as part of a 'return to myth' among twentieth-century writers generally, especially women writers:

> The experiences of black people in the New World, into which they have been forcibly thrust against their will, cannot be told or treated in realistic or naturalistic traditions in which American literature has been cast – the pain of the results of three centuries of oppression is too great to be faced and confronted in a realistic mode. (4)

A particular characteristic of the mythic narrative, then, is that it 'establishes lines to a world that is not only beyond the real world but that, at the same time, transforms it' (ibid., 4). *Tar Baby* uses a traditional African myth to project the reader beyond the conventional parameters of the contemporary in order to throw the complexities and tensions of the present into relief. In doing so the novel inverts and deconstructs a number of prior texts including the West African myth of Anaanu, the trickster spider to which we referred in the previous chapter, and the American vernacular tale of Brer Rabbit. As a fable, the tar baby story is supposed to reveal values but one of the ironies of the novel is that the values which are revealed are much more complex than those which underpinned the original oral narratives. As a result *Tar Baby* leads the reader not to a moral resolution, but to more complicated moral dilemmas.

The tar baby myth originated in Africa as part of a cycle of trickster tales associated with the spider, Anaanu, which developed before European contact. It reappeared in nineteenth-century America, initially as an African-American response to slavery but was then included by Joel Chandler Harris in his Uncle Remus plantation tales. Despite these different versions, the plot elements have changed very little. In the Uncle Remus version, Brer Fox sets the tar baby in the road to catch Brer Rabbit while he watches from the cover of the bushes. Brer Rabbit accuses the tar baby of being 'stuck up' and is determined to 'larn you howter talk ter 'specttubble folkes'. Angered by the tar baby's silence the rabbit strikes him and becomes stuck in the tar. In the version which Son tells, the tar baby is placed in the road by white farmers to entrap Brer Rabbit whom they believe is eating their cabbages. On finding the tar baby, Brer Rabbit is again offended by its apparent arrogance in not responding to his greeting; in the course of their encounter, the rabbit becomes entangled in the tar and completely immobilised. In this version, he is able to escape by manipulating the white farmers' cruelty, convincing them that he dreads being thrown into the briar patch from where he knows he will be able to escape. They cannot resist throwing him in because of their vindictiveness, evidencing the cruelty of whites generally towards others. However, as the tale evolves with each new version in a different context, the tar baby story acquires fresh meanings. As part of the African trickster cycle, the story is the tale of a scarecrow made out of sticky, gluey rubber to catch the trickster spider, Anaanu, which we associated with Macon Dead in the previous chapter. The scarecrow is constructed by Anaanu's family who are tired of seeing their yams disappear and it is the apparent haughtiness of the figure which, as in the Brer Rabbit version, arouses Anaanu to anger and results in him becoming entangled with it.

As one of the black oral tales of the plantations, Brer Rabbit encapsulates the wit and guile with which black slaves were able to outwit and survive the cruelty of their white masters. In *Tar Baby*, this strategy is employed by the black servant Gideon. Sydney, adopting the role of the superior black, presumes that Gideon, whom he calls by the name 'Yardman' rather than by his own name, is illiterate; Gideon for his part adopts this role to avoid being given the extra work which would follow if Sydney and Ondine knew he could read instructions. As a character in one of Harris's Uncle Remus tales, Brer Rabbit is drained of his guile and the story itself becomes an example of how white culture identified negroes with animals, in turn reconciling the inhuman treatment of black people with the whites' apparent Christian and democratic principles. Uncle Remus himself, a docile old slave who always wore a benign grin, became the white American stereotype of the acquiescent, faithful negro slave.

III

In *Tar Baby*, the various layers of meaning within the original African myth are reclaimed and adapted within a new cluster of significances for America, especially black America, in the late twentieth century. Brer Rabbit clearly re-enters the fable as the trickster figure, this time in the person of Son who, at the beginning of the novel, turns the household of Valerian Street upside down. Yet the text's concern with the way in which meanings are endlessly deferred ensures that Son is never quite reducible to Brer Rabbit even though the last paragraph of the novel makes the identification of the two explicit.

The enigmatic nature of Son is evident from the first and last episodes which frame the narrative. In the prologue to the novel, Son's plunge into the sea suggests not only death by drowning but also rebirth – he is 'yanked' into a wide, empty tunnel and finds himself 'whirling in a vortex'. At the end of the book, he emerges from the sea on to land in a sequence that mirrors the evolution of life; crawling, standing and eventually walking upright. In both episodes Son has a female guide. In the sea in the prologue he is kept afloat by the water spirit, 'like the hand of an insistent woman'. Suspending struggle, he gives in to the curent, 'the water-lady cupped him in the palm of her hand', and is guided to the boat, *Sea Bird 11*. As de Weever (1991) argues, the water spirit pushes Son into the adventure and by doing so shows her concern for the island and its inhabitants (37). In other words a supernatural female force enables Son to be born again out of the ocean to transform the lives of two women on the island about whom the ocean goddess would appear to be concerned. At the end of *Tar Baby*, Thérèse offers Son advice on negotiating the rocks and also warns him to keep away from Jadine because 'she has forgotten her ancient properties' (308). She immediately dissociates Jadine from the list of women, 'all of whom knew their true and ancient properties', to whom the novel is dedicated whilst associating herself with them. When Thérèse cuts the engine of the boat so that it moves with the tide, we are reminded of how he had been supported in the prologue by the water spirit. The implication that he has been singled out in some way is reinforced by the lifting mists which suggest the trees on the island are stepping back 'as if to make the way easier for a certain kind of man' (309).

The humour in the episode where Margaret Street reports Son to Valerian and Jadine sustains the mystery surrounding him because of her inability to find the right words to describe him; those she does use are misinterpreted or not understood at all. Like the trickster figures, of whom Brer Rabbit is one example, Son has lived on the edges of society. As Walker (1991) observes, the novel 'focuses on individuals who have cut their ties with community, family, and the past' (189) and Son is not only a veteran of Vietnam but also a fugitive who, having murdered his wife and her teenage lover, has been on the run for eight years. Changing his name several times, like the trickster figure, Son has assumed different identities among different peoples – William Green, Herbert Robinson, Louis Stover – and, in keeping with the trickster tradition, the reader never learns his true name. The fact that Son is a fugitive introduces another layer of complexity for he has to transform his own life and the lives of others as well. Like the other characters whose equilibrium, as the trickster figure, he disturbs, he has to learn that he cannot run away from his past. He is also more than a trickster figure in that he is, as Mbalia (1991) argues, 'a disciple for African people, a modern-day revolutionary' who has to realise that such powerful influences have permeated the African-American psyche that a doctrine of returning to a traditional African identity in an increasingly capitalist world is naïvely idealistic. He is also the skeleton in the Street's closet, both literally and metaphorically for he emerges from a wardrobe in their house. Black, bearded with 'chain-gang hair', he represents the African-American past which Valerian, as a white American capitalist, forgets, with which the black servants Sydney and Ondine have lost contact and which Jadine eschews. On one level he quite literally brings a family secret out in the open, the way in which Valerian's wife abused their son, Michael, when he was a small child by burning him with cigarettes. On another level he also brings the larger skeleton of the slave-past out of the closet for both Valerian and white America in general. In reporting Son's presence in the house to the others, the first thing Margaret says is that he is black. Valerian's candy factory uses sugar and cocoa, products of the Caribbean and of the slave system, a fact which Valerian and his black servant, Sydney, choose not to remember. In fact Valerian epitomises how so many members of the household retreat from the unpleasant facts of the negro past. His name associates him with a plant whose flowers are used medicinally as a sedative. As Mbalia (1991) says of him: he 'is asleep throughout most of his adult life, unconscious or unconcerned by the exploitive manner in which he has accumulated his wealth, ignorant of the physical and psychological abuse of his child by his own wife, unsympathetic to the feelings of his servants, and most important for Morrison and her audience, insensitive to the plight of African people' (70). Confronted with the image of the woman in yellow who spits at her, Jadine, who always averts her eyes from the ugly part of the island, takes a further leaf out of Valerian's book and literally buries her head under the pillow.

IV

The complexity of the novel derives from the way in which Jadine and Son are attracted to each other at the same time as each is repelled by the other. Each undergoes a process of transformation, initiated by the other; Son's appearance, for example, becomes increasingly European, he sports a borrowed white man's suit, cuts his hair and files his finger nails. The ambiguity in the novel is such that, as in the case of Son, Jadine is difficult to define as a signifier. If Son is ostensibly Brer Rabbit, then, in some respects, Jadine may be seen as a latter-day version of the tar baby itself. As the niece of Valerian's black servants, Sydney and Ondine, she has been educated with Valerian's financial support and is now a Europeanised African, an art history graduate of the Sorbonne in Paris, an expert on Cloisonné, and a cover model for *Elle*. The text develops in Jadine the haughtiness which is misunderstood in the original scarecrow and tar baby stories and which led to Anaanu and Brer Rabbit becoming entrapped. For Mbalia (1991), Jadine 'represents that which is inhuman, built by the European as a trap for other Africans, an artificial lure to tempt them to a Europeanized lifestyle' (75). In the course of the novel her association with tar assumes an increasingly wider significance. On revisiting the swamp after her return to the island from New York, her legs burn 'with the memory of tar'; her memory may be not only of a specific incident in her life but a folk memory of how tar was used to mask injuries to the skin of the slaves at auction. Yet throughout, Jadine's association with tar is ironic for she is lighter-skinned than this would suggest, significantly called 'Copper Venus'. Ondine's pride that Jadine has replaced a white model on the cover of *Elle* is especially ironic because she doesn't appreciate that Jadine has achieved this as a Europeanised version of black beauty; an irony compounded by the way Ondine stirs milk into the chocolate paste as she gloats over Jadine's triumph. Moreover at some points in the novel, Jadine appears to be a latter-day Brer Rabbit. Her experience of becoming trapped in the swamp in a substance which 'looks like pitch' is redolent of the experience of Brer Rabbit, for example, as is the way in which she becomes entangled with Son's image in her bedroom mirror: 'She struggled to pull herself away from his image in the mirror and to yank her tongue from the roof of her mouth' (113).

Despite the perceptive points they make, critics such as Mbalia

(1991) have tended to read the novel as a whole in terms of an oversimplified binary structure. Indeed one of Jadine's own faults, especially in the first half of the novel, is to see the world as consisting only of binary opposites. Mbalia, for example, maintains: 'What Morrison does in *Tar Baby* is raise the question all Africans must ask themselves: Do I identify with my oppressor or my people?' (68). This leads to some oversimplified interpretations:

> In fact, Jadine has so absorbed the capitalist values of making money and acquiring status that she is ignorant of the traditional African principles that have ensured the survival of African people despite their dehumanized conditions. Unequipped with a sense of humanism, collectivism, and egalitarianism to inform and guide her, she allows her aunt and uncle to wait on her, plays daughter to them instead of being daughter to them, and abandons them to the caprices of Valerian, not knowing what their fate might be. (75)

Such readings ignore the way in which the novel's concern with the endless deferment of meaning extends to issues of identity. In the novel identity is both externally multiple and internally fractured. As Derrida argued, all words/signs contain traces of the ones which have preceded them; every sign in a chain of meaning carries these traces in inexhaustible complexity. This is an idea which the novel pursues in relation to identity on a number of different levels. When Son, for example, gets into bed with Jadine in New York, his hands, 'large enough, maybe, to put your whole self into', also carry traces of the occasion when he held and kissed her bare foot, leaving fingerprints in its arch. When Jadine first encounters Son, she has difficulty determining what his hair signifies:

> Here, alone in her bedroom where there were no shadows, only glimmering unrelieved sunlight, his hair looked overpowering – physically overpowering, like bundles of long whips or lashes that could grab her and beat her to jelly. And would. Wild, aggressive, vicious hair that needed to be put in jail. Uncivilised, reform-school hair. Mau Mau, Attica, chain-gang hair. (113)

Similarly, the significance of the woman in yellow who spits contemptuously at Jadine eludes her attempts to define it. She almost becomes Jadine's tar baby – she has 'skin like tar against the canary yellow dress' – as Jadine becomes obsessed not so much with the woman as with her inability 'to fix the feeling that had troubled her' (45).

Despite the parallel concerns with *The Bluest Eye, Tar Baby* further complicates and defers the definition of African-American. Son makes the mistake of trying to define African-American identity in terms of an imposed traditional Africanism without recognising that at one level it offers little opportunity for growth and intellectual development, especially for black women. Traditional Africa is symbolised for Son by Eloe, but despite its positive qualities – collectivism and egalitarianism – it is a poor, underdeveloped and largely illiterate community. Although New York may be something of a packaged reality, yet another example of a second-hand existence in the novel, as Jadine observes: '. . . if there was a black woman's town, New York was it' (223). Son's estrangement from the blacks of New York is as much an indication of how far removed his ideas of black people are from theirs as it is a comment on the quality of their existences. In fact the description of New York on Son's arrival, emphasising the fact that all the black girls seem to be crying, all the black men seem to have dumped their blackness and that everyone walks looking straight ahead, casts Son in the mythical role of country mouse. Driven by such a singular perspective, it is less convincing than the account of Jadine's return to the city, enabling her legs to feel longer and her head to feel once more connected to her body. The space which is given in the novel to the cosmopolitan, eclectic nature of New York and Paris is a reminder that traditional boundaries of identity such as place, race, gender and class have become fractured by the flow of people, cultures, information and ideas across geographical frontiers. Eloe is emblematic of the ideal of wholeness, the ideal of the unified personality. But, as de Weever (1991) points out, such an ideal is not possible, and especially not for black women (173). In particular, young black women, the postmodern generation, often find themselves establishing identity within the fragmented personality they discover themselves inhabiting; for them life has to be 'lived between the cracks'.

V

The ambiguous position in which *Tar Baby* leaves Son and Jadine defers the kind of traditional closure which we might expect a novel to reach. Son is running into the rainforest where, according to one version of the myth, naked, blind men – slaves who escaped when the ship carrying them to the island floundered on the rocks – supposedly race horses over the hills whilst Jadine is left literally in mid-air on an aeroplane to Paris. The book appears to reclaim the open-ended conclusion of the Uncle Remus, Brer Rabbit and Brer Fox version of the tar baby tale. There we are not told the fate of Brer Rabbit; the story ends with him stuck to the tar and Brer Fox rolling on the ground with laughter, threatening to eat him. In response to the young boy to whom he told the story, Remus says inconclusively that 'some say Jedge B'ar come' long en loosed 'im – some say he didn't'. The unresolved nature of the novel's ending might encourage readers to review the narrative, creating their own scenarios of what is going to happen to Son and Jadine, either individually or together. A teleological conclusion to a novel normally makes sense to the reader when the parts that lead up to it are re-examined in hindsight. But the conclusion of this novel possibly serves only to make the reader more aware of how much in the text is deferred, for as one critic, Craig H. Werner, has argued, 'the style and texture of *Tar Baby* emphasize multiplicity' (McKay, 1988, 156). Whilst Valerian interprets the island as a bastion of European culture, a stay against chaos, Son thinks only of its oppressive racial history, anticipating the concern in *Beloved*, the next novel, with reclaiming repressed and unvoiced narratives.

Parallels within the novel invite the reader to compare similar episodes, but such comparisons often serve only to compound ambiguity and ambivalence of meaning. The swamp-women whom Jadine thinks she sees while pulling herself from the green, tar-like slime have difficulty, like Margaret and Jadine on first seeing Son, interpreting what they are witnessing. At first they mistake Jadine for a runaway child who has been returned to them; but then it appears she might be struggling to escape them. The swamp-women themselves offer the reader a similar level of difficulty of interpretation. The swamp-women are echoed in the night-women who visit Jadine in a waking dream in Eloe and who include Son's dead mother, Ondine, Thérèse and her own mother. They appear to represent traditional black womanhood, if not motherhood, which Jadine denies and from which she is running away. There is much evidence to support this interpretation. The fact that Jadine, the daughter of Sydney's dead sister, is orphaned appears to serve as a symbol of her disconnectedness from her ancestral mothers and it is this discontinuity which some critics believe the woman in yellow who spits at Jadine observes in her. Here Morrison appears to draw upon an African concept in which ancestors are believed to take an active interest in the welfare of their living descendants, intervening in their lives to remind them of their culturally specific moral obligations. Once again the myth is complicated and made problematic by its appropriation in the novel.

One of the distinctions between Jadine and the woman in yellow, who is also one of Jadine's night-women, is the difference between their bodies. Jadine has a slim, model's frame but she observes that the woman in yellow has 'too much hip, too much bust' (42). Indeed all the night-women symbolically reveal their child-bearing breasts to Jadine while the woman in yellow offers her three eggs, further emblems of femaleness, fertility and motherhood; their action recalls Son's jaundiced suspicions that 'her breast tip [sic] were tiny brass knobs like those ornately carved fixtures screwed into the drawers of Jadine's writing table' (197). Jadine's rejection of the night-women does betray her fear of them: '. . . folded stomachs, they seemed somehow in agreement with each other about her, and were all out to get her, tie her, bind her. Grab the person she had worked hard to become and choke it off with their soft loose tits' (264).

Nevertheless, an interpretation which focuses on Jadine's denial of her black womanhood is here complicated by the fact that Jadine wants for herself roles other than those which black women have traditionally held. Critics such as Mbalia (1991) have observed Jadine's arrogant failure to acknowledge what black women have achieved even within these (81). But her reaction to the night-women has to be placed in the context of her full experience of Eloe. Jadine's desire to achieve different roles for herself is reinforced by her recognition that Eloe offers few challenges or opportunities for fulfilment, intellectual or sexual, for black women:

Eloe was rotten and more boring than ever. A burnt-out place. There was no life there. Maybe a past but definitely no future and finally there was no interest. All that Southern small-town country romanticism was a lie, a joke, kept secret by people who could not function elsewhere. (262)

Her frustrations over the place jar with Son's enthusiasm which is emphasised in the repetition of the line: 'Yet he insisted on Eloe'. Ironically, despite Son's association with the female insect which fertilises plants – he pinches Valerian's cyclamen so that it blossoms – he is a woman killer. Werner (McKay, 1988) explains how:

> Holding to the folk myth of the white world as a tar baby, Son creates a complementary myth of Eloe as briar patch . . . His myth of safety in the briar patch evades the risk of his relationship with Jadine. By embracing a myth that dehistoricizes Jadine's complex history as a black woman, he increases the possibility of suffering the loss he most fears. (164–5)

It is too simple to conclude, as Mbalia does, that Jadine is a negative character because she has embraced capitalism:

> Jadine kissed his hands and he asked her why she left the States in the first place. She said she always thought she had three choices: marry a dope king or a doctor, model, or teach art at Jackson High. In Europe she thought there might be a fourth choice. They told each other everything. Yet he insisted on Eloe. (226)

The text avoids reducing Jadine/Son and Jadine/night-women to a singular narrative constructed around pairs of binary opposites in the same way that the observation that the swamp-women were arrogant precludes any singular interpretation of them. As Eleanor W. Traylor points out:

> These women, by allusion, figure the warrior women, the market women, the calabash-carrying women, the queen women, the life-bearing, culture-bearing women of their ancient origins. (McKay, 1988, 149)

VI

Despite her obvious faults, Jadine, like Sula, is an independently-minded and sexually-liberated woman whom the novel, in places, invites us to admire as we are asked at times to favour Sula. Mbalia's (1991) criticism that Jadine insults the Eloens by sleeping naked within view of them is rather simplistic (81). Apart from the fact that she finds the heat of her room stifling, Jadine is accustomed to sleeping naked, an index of her liberated sexuality. The night-women make her feel obscene in her nakedness, denying her the liberation she has achieved in Paris and New York, whilst Soldier expects her to be submissive and accepting of his sexism. His insensitive description of Son's wife as having had 'the best pussy in Florida', together with the way in which he naturally presumes to ask if Jadine has children, and his interest in who is in control in the relationship between Jadine and Son present us with the restrictiveness of Eloe. Soldier is both disturbed and attracted by Jadine's spirit and independence – 'You a hot one, ain't you' – and the text significantly explores the nature of her sexual independence in her relationship with Son before she arrives in Eloe to encounter the censorship of the night-women:

> Jadine was so ruttish by the time she got to the Hilton, she could barely stand still for the doorman to take her bags, and when she was checked in, and had gotten his room number from information, she did not call him – she took the elevator to his floor and banged on the door. When he opened it, she jumped on him with her legs around his waist crashing him into the purple carpet. (224)

The passage conflates Jadine's independence and her sexual confidence. Like Sula, she is prepared to take the initiative and seeks sexual satisfaction for herself in relationships unlike women such as Nel who suppress their own needs and desires in order to appease their men.

If the text suggests that Son's view of Eloe is not to be trusted then Son's view of Jadine must also be open to question, as later in his dream of their life together and in his view of New York. When Jadine balks because she thinks that Son is about to rape her, he accuses her of embracing the white stereotype of the African: 'Rape? Why you little white girls always think somebody's trying to rape you?' (121). Mbalia (1991) sees this as evidence of how Jadine thinks like a European (72). However, Son responds not so much to what she says as to her assertiveness. When she protests at being called white, his response – 'Then why don't you settle down and stop acting like it' – ignores the content and focuses on her behaviour. Jadine is not simply responding to being found out by a black man as someone who has betrayed her race; she is reacting to a black man who appears to deny her right to think for herself. She threatens to kill him for 'pulling that black-woman-white-woman shit' on her and for thinking he can 'get away' with telling her 'what a black woman is or ought to be' (121). Son is incensed by Jadine not only because she is Europeanised, but because she has not accepted the traditional role of a black woman, accusing her of getting where she has purely on the basis of sexual favours. Confessing to Jadine the details of how he killed his wife, Son enjoys her fear and is said to 'bask in it like a cat in steam-pipe heat' (178). Towards her he feels at the same time protective and violent, both, in different ways, behaviours which have as much to do with power in relationships as desire. In New York, while waiting to meet again with Jadine, Son has very traditional dreams of their life together. Apparently forgetting her education and career plans, and that he is a fugitive, Son thinks of himself earning the money to keep them while Jadine will have their baby. He thinks of the child, significantly, as his son whom he contemplates naming after himself.

Of course there are criticisms to be made of Jadine as there are of Sula and the novel also demonstrates her weaknesses. She is hard, as her name suggests, and self-indulgent, seeking only to live in the present, eschewing her obligations to others and turning her back on her ancestral line. Her commitment to her own individual fulfilment rather than to a sense of solidarity with other black people is evident in her favouring of the interpretation of the mythic horse riders on the island told her by a neighbour; that rather than a hundred ex-slaves there is only one French soldier on a horse. Her surname, Childs, indicates that Jadine is, in different ways, as immature as Son who is accused by Jadine of thinking 'like a kid' and whose name emphasises that he has failed to wean himself away from Eloe. It is because of these failings that Son and Rosa in Eloe are able to make her feel ashamed as if what repulses her is inside herself and not in them. But even this is presented in the novel with considerable ambiguity. The account of Rosa's observation of Jadine's nakedness conveys not so much disgust and embarrassment, as Mbalia (1991) argues, but interest in Jadine's body itself. The passage takes almost as long to read as Rosa's eyes take to pass down Jadine, recalling how Valerian let his eyes 'travel cautiously' down the full length of Son's body on first seeing him, thus casting the reader into the role of voyeur:

> Rosa gazed down Jadine's body with a small bowing of her head, and then up again. Her eyes travelled slowly, moving like one of those growing plants Jadine could not see, but whose presence was cracking loud. (254)

The kind of complexity demonstrated by the relationship between Son and Jadine and the apparent contradictions in their characters have been underemphasised by critics. As Butler-Evans (1989) has noted, critics of Morrison's novels, not specifically *Tar Baby*, have tended to interpret 'the works as nonproblematic bodies of fiction' and have inferred 'univocal meaning' (60). She points out how, with the exception of Barbara Christian (1985), they have often focused on the symbolic constructions of a black community, whilst ignoring how the desires of black women are seldom realised there (61). The tensions in Morrison's novels between feminine desires and community needs are often, as in *Tar Baby*, left not so much unnegotiated as in the process of negotiation. Jadine has to work through for herself the significance of the night-women; she cannot now simply reject them. Unable to give up the ambitions which drive her to realise herself, to define herself on her own terms rather than according to traditional black definitions of womanhood, to her the night-women are a reminder of the black female ancestry which is there for her to acknowledge without necessarily re-enacting. As Werner argues, Jadine 'will not simply create a new second-order myth repressing the reality of her past experience' (165). The description of the last sight we have of Jadine reinforces the increasing difficulty she is having in being so single-minded. The repetition of the line – 'There is no time for dreaming' – and the self-sacrifice of the soldier ants undermine Jadine's solipsism, indicating that she may yet negotiate the conflicting discourses to which she is subject in order to find fulfilment in all aspects of her life. The section concludes in a way that suggests this may be the case: 'Still it would be hard. So very hard to forget the man who fucked like a star' (294). Jadine resolves to confront the 'funkiness' which she has denied, together with dreams and death. The novel avoids the cliché whereby a single-minded woman of independent means capitulates, tamed by a man whose values are made out in the end to be morally superior to hers, and who it is revealed in hindsight wanted all along, despite the conflicts, for him to bring her under his control. Although Son sets out to find Jadine, his attitude to Eloe has been changed by her. Significantly in trying to reclaim for himself what he once found in the women there he looks at photographs of the night-women of Eloe taken, and therefore mediated, by Jadine:

> Gazing at the photos one by one trying to find in them what it was
> that used to comfort him so, used to reside with him, in him like

royalty in his veins. . . . It all looked miserable in the photographs, sad, poor and even poor-spirited. (296–7)

Although not in any conclusive or simple way, both Jadine and Son have been propelled into a process of some kind of transformation; appropriately, for islands, as de Weever (1991) reminds us, have a significant association in Western culture as 'places of transformation' and they have 'acquired an almost numinous quality' (45). The inconclusiveness of these respective transformations, concomitant with the reclamation of open-ended mythic narratives, highlights the complex process by which black people, especially black women, have to negotiate the competing discourses which influence individual and cultural behaviour. In *Tar Baby*, the classic concept of the individual with a solid, coherent identity is eschewed for a model of identity which sees the individual as a kaleidoscope of heterogeneous impulses and desires, constructed from multiple forms of interaction with the world as a play of difference that cannot be completely comprehended.

6

Beloved (1987)

I

Any novel is a transposition of material from different sources – both literary and non-literary. Whilst Roland Barthes, the French theorist, overstates the case in suggesting that authors can only combine existing texts, he astutely observes how 'bits of codes, formulae, rhythmic models, fragments of social languages, etc. pass into text and are redistributed within it' (Barthes, 1981, 39). His concept of a given text as a point of intersection for a range of different discourses is particularly appropriate to *Beloved* which the reader may feel is the most fragmentary of Morrison's novels. This chapter explores the nature of this fragmentation and the experience which *Beloved* offers the reader.

At one level *Beloved* is a romance between Sethe and Paul D, two ex-slaves reunited in post-Civil War America. The historical context makes their relationship special, for under slavery black people were not allowed to have free physical and emotional relationships and as such their relationship becomes part of the healing process which Morrison hoped that the novel would provide. However, their reunion is problematised by the relationships of each of them to Sethe's children, one of whom is a ghost incarnate of the child murdered by Sethe. Both of them are haunted by their pasts and dehumanised by what they have done or what has been done to them.

Of all Morrison's novels, *Beloved* most obviously illustrates Joanne Braxton's assertion that female slave narratives planted the seed of contemporary Black feminist and 'womanist' writing early in the Black literary tradition (Braxton and McLaughlin, 1990, 302). As we said in the introduction, the novel is loosely based on the story of Mary Garner, a slave who killed her child and attempted to kill herself rather

93

than return to slavery. Set in 1873, the book, like Morrison's earlier works, moves from the present to the past, particularly the period 1850–1855, and back again. As in her first novel, single events are revisited from different viewpoints in a narrative which employs both first and third person perspectives. However, these characteristic techniques of Morrison's work acquire a special edge in this novel which explores how authoritative discourses – for example, historical, biblical, cultural, and political accounts – bury alternative interpretations, thus serving to silence other voices.

In some respects *Beloved* draws upon the black aesthetic discourse of the 1960s in which, as Butler-Evans (1989) points out, narratives as oppositional or alternative texts posited self-reconstruction and redefinition through deconstructing Western assumptions about blackness (26). A preoccupation with unearthing narratives which have been hidden by or buried within other narratives is integral to the structure of *Beloved* in which there are two interrelated levels of occlusion: the white distortion of black experience and the suppressed subconscious. The latter is pursued in the novel at the level of the individual, most obviously Sethe, but also at the level of white America's need to confront what it has done to black people and to itself.

II

The main events of *Beloved* constitute Sethe's past which the reader has to construct piecemeal and which Sethe herself tries to avoid: 'As for the rest, she worked hard to remember as close to nothing as was safe' (6). The backbone of the novel is an occluded text buried within the surface narrative which the reader has to recover in order to make sense of the whole, as Sethe has to reclaim it also to understand the main events of her life. These events include the death of her mother; her marriage to Halle; a whipping which almost kills her; her escape and refuge in the home of her mother-in-law; her recapture and the infanticide of her child; her period of imprisonment; the subsequent years in 124; her sons – Howard and Buglar – being driven away from there by the ghost of Beloved, the child she killed; her years in an all-female household where the third member is a ghost-daughter. There are, however, further narratives which have to be reclaimed which include the horrors of slavery itself. As Gates, Jr (1992) reminds us, 'accused of lacking a formal and collective history, blacks published individual histories which, taken together, were intended to narrate, in segments, the larger yet fragmented history of blacks in Africa, now dispersed throughout a cold New World' (62). By employing this method in *Beloved*, Morrison thought of herself as writing in response to a significant absence. In an interview with Paul Gilroy (1993), she argues: 'Slavery wasn't in the literature at all. Part of that, I think, is, because, on moving from bondage into freedom which has been our goal, we got away from slavery and also from the slaves, there's a difference. We have to re-inhabit those people' (179). When Paul D, a fellow slave, turns up after eighteen years and drives out the spirit ghost of Beloved, she returns as a young woman intent on separating Sethe and Paul D in order to claim her mother for herself. But she is more than Sethe's daughter-incarnate; she is also Sethe's personal past and the past of slavery which Sethe has to reclaim. In the second part of the novel there are three acts of identification – Sethe claims Beloved as her daughter-incarnate, Denver claims Beloved as her sister and Beloved claims Sethe as her mother – emblematic of America's need to identify and confront the narratives of black history; the novel is, after all, dedicated to 'sixty million and more'.

Beloved begins with Sethe remembering some of the above-mentioned events which she would rather forget. But it is clear to the reader from the very nature of them that not only can she not forget them but that she needs to remember and confront them. This is obvious in the memory of her dying baby's wound which she herself has inflicted. But there are other suppressed memories including the way in which she had to have sex with an engraver in order to pay to have the word 'Beloved' on the baby's tombstone. The fact that she will not be able to move on until she has come to terms with her past is especially evident from the 'thought pictures' which haunt her of the young men hanging from the trees in the plantation ironically called 'Sweet Home'. Within this context Paul D's sudden arrival seems predestined: 'As if to punish her further for her terrible memory, sitting on the porch not forty feet away was Paul D, the last of the Sweet Home men' (6). Sethe's account to him of how Baby Suggs died nine years previously sets the tone of much of the novel; '[Her death was] Soft as cream. Being alive was the hard part' (7). Sethe's attempt to come to terms with everything is inevitably painful. Early in the novel she fleetingly remembers words spoken by Amy, the poor white daughter of an unindentured servant who helped her when she escaped from the plantation: 'Anything dead coming back to life hurts' (35). Later in the book, when Amy's nursing of Sethe for two days is described in detail, her words of reassurance appear to be directed at the reader who by this time has read in piecemeal of the horrors of slavery: 'Good for you. More it hurt more better it is. Can't nothing heal without pain, you know. What you wiggling for?' (78). Paul D is as reluctant as Sethe to confront the past; indeed in some respects he is more unwilling to do so, believing that he has locked up the past for good in the tobacco tin he carries around his neck:

> It was some time before he could put Alfred, Georgia, Sixo, schoolteacher, Halle, his brother, Sethe, Mister, the taste of iron, the sight of butter, the smell of hickory, notebook paper, one by one, into the tobacco tin lodged in his chest. By the time he got to 124 nothing in this world could pry it open. (113)

Ironically the lid is prised open by something supernatural, the ghost of Beloved in the form of a young woman. As she seduces him, he does not hear the flakes of rust fall from the seams and the lid eventually gives. The pain and horror which he has kept sealed for so long is eventually released in his escalating and repetitive cry, 'Red heart', which eventually wakes Denver.

III

Whilst *Beloved* is clearly indebted to Black Aesthetic discourse of the 1960s, it would be misleading to suggest that the influence is so strong that it posits the novel solely in opposition to white Western discourse. The novel pursues possibilities arising out of black literary and cultural traditions, especially the symbols and forms of the experience of black women themselves. Like *The Bluest Eye*, *Beloved*, as a development of the Mary Garner story, is concerned with the conditions that lead a parent to commit an act of violence against their child. In the former novel, as we saw earlier, Cholly Breedlove's rape of his daughter is the result of the guilt and impotence which has been imposed on him by a society which declares him worthless. The reasons for Sethe's actions, however, are even more complex than in Cholly's case, and the horrific event cannot be separated from the slave system which destroyed so many black lives. *Beloved* subverts the white myth of Southern paternalism in which the slave owners were envisaged as presiding over an extended and subservient family of both black and white. Whilst this narrative was constructed from the South's supposed commitment to family, honour, good manners, culture, and order, the reality had more to do with property and ownership. In self-justification of slavery, the South perpetuated the illusion of a system as stable as its 'Big Houses', in which everyone including master, overseer, house slaves, Mammies and field slaves had their place, eschewing the realities of forced labour and servitude, the mundane brutality of plantation life, and the destruction of black families. Sethe's decision to kill her child rather than have her taken into slavery has to be seen in the context of her past. Only a month previously she had endured an almost fatal whipping and suffered the degradation of being chained while the white men sucked her lactating breasts. After a month with Baby Suggs, Sethe's recapture and return to the plantation would have been too much for anyone in her position. Her own version of what happened stands in contrast to the other narratives of her child's death in the novel including that in the newspaper which Stamp Paid gives to Paul D:

> Simple. She just flew. Collected every bit of life she had made, all the parts of her that were precious and fine and beautiful, and carried, pushed, dragged them through the veil, out, away, over there where no one could hurt them. Over there. Outside this place, where they would be safe. And the hummingbird wings beat on. (163)

On many different levels throughout *Beloved*, Morrison is concerned with texts that lie beyond or are occluded by authoritative versions. Sethe blames only herself for the murder of her child until her mother-in-law, Baby Suggs, points out to her that the real responsibility lies with white people and the inhumane system they have imposed upon blacks: 'Those white things have taken all I had or dreamed,' she [Baby Suggs] said, 'and broke my heart strings too. There is no bad luck in the world but whitefolks' (89). In other words Baby Suggs introduces Sethe to an alternative text from the one with which she has lived since killing her child. Alternative texts are also developed around Baby Suggs' life. Stamp Paid blames her for abandoning her life as a preacher in 1855, that is for privileging self-interested individualism over collective needs. But he comes to see her as a strong woman defeated by whites and to appreciate how she might have felt when the women of the community which she served brought about the death of her daughter-in-law. Denver, Sethe's 18 year old daughter with whom she has lived alone for some years in a house haunted by the ghost of the baby she killed, has a view of white people which later observations change. Denver has been brought up on Sethe's narrative of how she had been helped by Amy Denver after whom Denver is named and presumes that the majority of white people are like her rather than the slave owners. Although Miss Bodwin helps Denver and prepares her for college, she ruthlessly exploits her black servant and provides the most obvious counterpoint to Denver's view of white people. Moreover in the statue of a kneeling black boy at Miss Bodwin's back door, bearing the words 'At Yo Service', Denver encounters a visual text which underpins the way in which whites regarded the black race. It is a perspective to which Baby Suggs in her sermons in the clearing offers a counterpoint, encouraging pride and self-esteem among the members of her community: 'Love your hands! Love them! Raise them up and kiss them. Touch others with them . . . *You* got to love it, *you*' (88). Indeed the meetings in the clearing provide a much-needed opportunity for them since, as we said at the outset, plantation practices prevented black people from having relationships or even speaking together. As Lomax (1962) argues:

> By listening and fervently responding to the pure poetry of the Negro preacher, the Negro masses got a sense of history and moral philosophy. There is something incredibly informative about sitting Sunday after Sunday and year in, year out, listening to a minister trace out the history of the Jews from the day God spit out the seven seas to the time John the Revelator closed the Bible and said all truth had been revealed. Even those of us who couldn't read came to think of history as a moving, changing thing; we were never allowed to doubt that man as a created thing had purpose and that we, to be sure, were a part of that purpose. (47)

Baby Suggs, like other preachers, gave the slave community, as Lomax suggests, a context in which it could place itself and which could act as a refuge and source of strength. She is an example of what Braxton identifies as the outraged female ancestor, angry at the abuse of her people and feeling keenly every wrong done to them (Braxton and McLaughlin, 1990, 302).

Beloved particularly reclaims a number of occluded narratives around slavery, including its rejection of a popularly accepted notion that slaves were treated well on some plantations; a 'text' which Mr Garner tries to invoke when Baby Suggs' son, Halle, eventually manages to buy his mother from slavery. As Baby Suggs points out to Mr Garner, slavery is slavery no matter how the slaves are treated. In African-American culture, the North itself became a text, as is evident from Paul D's conception of it when he leaves the Cherokees: 'From North. Magical North. Welcoming, benevolent North' (112). Once again it is ironic because the reality of the North was far from welcoming and benevolent. The final tableau of the novel in which Sethe attacks the white abolitionist, Edward Bodwin, Miss Bodwin's brother, with an ice pick is especially ironic in this respect. She mistakes Bodwin, who has come to 124 to give Denver a ride to work, for a slave catcher. Although literally false, Sethe's assumption is emblematic, at another level, of black history after the Civil War, as Walker argues (1991, 43). When Stamp Paid pulls a red ribbon from the river connected to a piece of a young black girl's scalp, he recovers another narrative, as it were – the way in which emancipation brought not freedom but the widespread slaughter of former slaves. If death did not catch them, there was little by way of opportunity for the ex-slaves. When the Federal troops were withdrawn in 1877, the blacks were left materially, socially, educationally and politically impoverished. Of the threequarters of them who remained in the Southern states, the majority of them were in agriculture, locked into a semi-feudal system of tenancy or share-cropping which replaced the slave plantations. The impotence of many of the white liberals to deliver the promise of emancipation is illustrated in the way in which Edward Bodwin constructs a text of his own past as an abolitionist – 'Nothing since was as stimulating as the old days of letters, petitions, meetings, debates, recruitment, quarrels, rescue and downright sedition' (260) – serving to underscore the paucity of his present which is epitomised in the image of a man searching for toy soldiers and a watch he had long ago buried in the yard of 124.

Morrison's interest in occluded texts around the subject of slavery is evident from her use of the Bible. In *Beloved*, the words which Sethe uses to claim Beloved – 'Beloved she mine' – and which Beloved used to claim Sethe – 'I am Beloved and she is mine' – have their source in *The Song of Solomon* which had inspired the title and, in part, the concern with ancestral wisdom in her earlier novel. The epigraph of *Beloved* reminds us that its title comes from a part of Paul's epistle to the Romans in which he in turn is quoting Hosea in the Old Testament. One of Hosea's three children was called 'not beloved', a representative of the Israelites who had been temporarily rejected as punishment for their own betrayal. After a period of retribution, God reclaims the lost people:

> I will call them my people,
> which were not my people;
> and her beloved,
> which was not beloved.

On the plantations religious instruction was used as a form of social control. The Bible, read from a particular historicised, cultural perspective, was one of the means by which colonial authorities tried to inculcate Western values and introduce European or Anglo-European notions of culture to Africa. Indeed its apparent dualism – 'Black Satan' and 'the snow-white Lamb of God' – appeared not only to justify slavery, but to offer up the history of slavery as a particular text, as it were. The Bible like all texts is not just one text but a multi-layered narrative. Interpreted from a black perspective, it could be seen as a different text from that which had been used by whites to justify slavery providing images appropriate to their condition and history: delivery of the Righteous, retribution of the Wicked, Judgement day, Zion, the Promised Land. Through its delineation of the history of the Jewish nation, the Bible expounded the trials and miseries of slavery. It offered slaves a source of communal strength through notions of faith, grace and the Holy Spirit, even a means of achieving healing.

IV

In locating the title of *Beloved* in the Bible, critics such as Walker (1991) have failed to pursue the implication that African-American writers have gone to a different text, a different Bible, from whites. Yet, as we have tried to show, it is a thesis that actually highlights a major concern in the novel with reclaiming occluded or absent texts. Indeed it is the absent text around the word 'beloved' that highlights the political message of the book. The source of the word 'beloved' is not only in Paul's epistle to the Romans, but in the words spoken by the preacher over Beloved's grave. Sethe, who bought the name for her daughter's gravestone with ten minutes of stand-up sex with the stone engraver, would have liked to have had the other word – 'Dearly' – which the preacher spoke over her dead child. As Walker (1991) points out, there were other words too: 'we are gathered here together. . . .' These words clearly and obviously draw attention to the main subject of the novel: the reclamation of a sense of community and solidarity in the face of fragmentation and isolation.

As we suggested at the outset, Sethe's healing and rebirth can only begin when she has knowledge and understanding of the absent narratives. The novel hinges upon what is called rememory, the basic concept of which is that memories have a physical existence beyond the minds of the individuals in whom they originate: it is possible to bump into and inhabit another person's memory. Paul D is associated with rememory throughout the novel. At the beginning of the book, he brings to Sethe rememories of what happened to her husband, Halle, and explanations as to why he did not come to console her. Sethe literally learns to inhabit and take for herself these rememories which are Paul's. In doing so, she begins to piece things together and Sethe's experience in this respect mirrors the experience of the reader in tackling the intricately woven structure of the novel as a whole. At the end of the novel, for example, just before Paul D returns to reclaim Sethe from death, he is haunted by something he does not understand, something on the edge of consciousness. Suddenly, he realises that it is a memory of Baby Suggs dying, although the memory is not his own because she died nine years earlier, in his absence. Such shifts between different narrative levels and challenges to ideas of causality are techniques used by Morrison to represent a sense of community in the novel. One of the concluding images is of Paul beside Sethe's bed, rocking and staring at the patchwork quilt. The novel itself is like a quilt and it is important to remember that the quilt, a feminine art form, was used to map the ancestry of a family as each successive generation added to it.

The concept of rememory and the notion of a repossessed ancestry are inextricably woven together. The privileging of memory by African-American writers is a political as well as an aesthetic project. As Gates, Jr (1992), points out, the white lie that black people did not have a memory was encouraged as part of the myth that black people and American Indians had lower mental capacities than other races. As he observes 'metaphors of the "childlike" nature of the slaves, of the masked, puppetlike "personality" of the black, all share this assumption about the absence of memory' (61). Typical of this viewpoint is the way in which a novelist, Mary Langdon, writing in 1855, described blacks as 'mere children . . . You seldom hear them say much about anything that's past, if they only get enough to eat and drink at the present moment' (cit. Gates, Jr, 1992, 62). But in fact the connection between rememory and the reclamation of ancestry, racial pride and self-esteem is much deeper than even Gates, Jr, suggests. The idea of rememory, as defined in *Beloved*, could only have originated with a dispossessed people. Since slavery destroyed not only whole communities but entire families, banning their religions, stopping their music and eradicating their cultures, the only way in which individuals could acquire any sense of their ancestral line was to possess and piece together the stories and memories of others, to literally acquire for themselves the texts of which they had been deprived. The full significance and the extent of the fracture which slavery created for black people can only be appreciated in the light of the African concept of ancestry. In African cosmology ancestors are important because they provide access to the spirits who intrude for the benefit of social cohesiveness into people's lives. Obliterating black slaves' contact with their ancestors thus also destroyed their contact with the spirits. Through its powerful figurative language, the novel impresses the enormity of this fracture on the reader. The fragmentary nature of the novel means that even if readers succeed in putting together the events of Sethe's life since 1855, it will not allow them to achieve a grasp of the whole text.

The sense of fracture which is at the heart of the book – together with a concomitant sense of healing – is maintained, if not actually initiated, by the slippage of the signifier 'Beloved' throughout the novel. On one level Beloved subverts the notion of the outraged mother figure as an outraged ghost-daughter intent upon claiming the mother who killed her for herself alone, but she eludes precise definition. At first she appears to be the spirit ghost of the murdered baby, but no sooner has the reader acquired this hold on her than she reappears, or seems to reappear, in the form of a young woman. Eventually she appears to represent not a single child but the pain and anguish of the 60 million blacks who have been enslaved, tortured and killed. As a character, then, Beloved is commensurate with the fantastical in African literature which is usually traceable back to concrete, social and historical events. But Beloved moves from one plane of reference to another, literally destabilising the novel which also moves with an equally destabilising effect from one narrative plane to another. This destabilising is central to the novel because just as Morrison's creative use of the Bible in the epigraph exemplifies how African-American writers find an 'African' text in the white man's religious book, *Beloved* reminds us of other texts inside the narrative of slavery which have come down to us by white male or black male chroniclers. It presents us with a black woman's version of slavery as a counterpoint to a narrative that has until now been told from a male point of view. This is made clear when Stamp Paid visits 124 and hears, undecipherable to him, 'the thoughts of the women of 124, unspeakable thoughts, unspoken' (199). The black centre of the novel, associated with the spiritual and with healing, expounds the pain, humiliation and violence endured and, in many cases, transcended by generations of black women.

It is no coincidence that the two main healers in the novel, Baby Suggs and Amy, are women and that Paul D, one of the most sympathetically portrayed black men in Morrison's work, is associated with the feminine. The reader is given an insight into the caring nature of Paul D when his first thought on hearing of Baby Suggs' death is: 'Was it hard? I hope she didn't die hard' (7). At the end of the novel, Sethe, wondering whether Paul will bathe her, recalls:

> She looks at him. The peachstone skin, the crease between his ready, waiting eyes and sees it – the thing in him, the blessedness, that has made him the kind of man who can walk in a house and make the women cry. (272)

These lines are a repetition of the omniscient narrator's description of Paul D when he first visits and makes love with Sethe:

> Not even trying, he had become the kind of man who could walk into a house and make the women cry. Because with him, in his presence, they could. There was something blessed in his manner. Women saw him and wanted to weep – to tell him that their chest hurt and their knees did too. Strong women and wise saw him and told him things they only told each other: that way past the Change of Life, desire in them had suddenly become enormous, greedy, more savage than when they were fifteen, and that it embarrassed them and made them sad; that secretly they longed to die – to be quit of it – that sleep was more precious to them than any waking day. Young girls sidled up to him to confess or describe how well-dressed the visitations were that had followed them straight from their dreams. (17)

When sitting rocking at the end of the novel, Paul recalls Amy who rocked Sethe's pain as she lay beside her recalling how her own mother sang as she rocked.

The account of how Paul has a special affinity with women is a glimpse into a further text rooted in the interior life of black woman. In piecing together the structure of the novel we weave this text together as well; a text so inextricably a part of the novel as to give the language of the book its particular charge. This is evident, for example, in Sethe's account of her own mother to Beloved:

> I didn't see her but a few times out in the fields and once when she was working indigo. By the time I woke up in the morning, she was in line. If the moon was bright they worked by its light. Sunday she slept like a stick. She must of nursed me two or three weeks – that's the way the others did. Then she went back in rice and I sucked from another woman whose job it was. So to answer you, no. I reckon not. She never fixed my hair nor nothing. She didn't even sleep in the same cabin most nights I remember. Too far from the line-up, I guess. (60–1)

For the women to be forced to work by the light of the traditional symbol of the female underlines the brutalisation of their identity as women. The use of the verb 'sucked' emphasises how the white man's system has reduced black women to breeding stock – as does the stealing of Sethe's milk. Coupled with the noun 'job', it also reinforces the denial of the closest of emotional bonds, that between mother and child, and how slavery exploits post-natal rejection by turning the separation of mother and child into a systemised form of breeding. 'Line' and 'line-up' emphasise the factory-like nature of the system while betraying its role in supporting a capitalist, industrial society. The inclusion of the word 'stick' is effective not only in completing the consonance, but in emphasising the life-denying nature of the whole process. A stick, like a slave, has been broken off from its life source and is thereby dry and dead. Paul D eventually comes to realise that in listening to Sethe he has made the mistake of hearing a traditional narrative – 'This here Sethe talked about love like any other woman; talked about baby clothes like any other woman. . . .' – whilst in fact she 'talked about safety with a handsaw' and 'didn't know where the world stopped and she began' (164).

Mothering and motherhood were denied, devalued and obliterated by slavery since black women were regarded as breeding stock. The novel takes us, as Christian says, into the chaotic space of mother-love and mother-pain in which a mother kills her child in order to save it (Braxton and McLaughlin, 1990, 338–9). Here Morrison uses a different context to develop a subject touched upon in *Sula* where Eva kills Plum, who has returned from the First World War a narcotics addict, because she cannot stand to see him suffer any longer. *Beloved* pushes at the very boundaries of this chaotic space; when Sethe tells Paul D about how they stole her milk, the horror of what happened is such that it causes him to handle the pouch containing the tobacco tin, fearing it will bring forth everything that he believes he has sealed away. Her account brings to the fore, uncompromisingly, the bond between mother and child which slavery destroyed:

> All I knew was I had to get my milk to my baby girl. Nobody was going to nurse her like me. Nobody was going to get it to her fast enough, or take it away when she had enough and didn't know it. (16)

The song which Amy sings to ease Sethe's pain conflates mother-love with mother-pain; combining tenderness with vicarious suffering. The memory of the song and of the way in which her mother used to sing to her highlights the absence of her mother. Yet it is her remembered presence which enables Amy to bind with and heal Sethe, saving her and her child from certain death. The narrative we have at this point in the novel is the one which Denver relates to Beloved, fleshing out scraps of information which she had gleaned from her mother. The narrative, which is Sethe's narrative, brings Denver and Beloved together, as Amy's recollection of her mother unites her and Sethe.

The denial and obliteration of motherhood and mothering distort the notion of womanhood in Morrison's work which is reclaimed, as best as it can be, at several points in the novels by a reclamation of the mother–child bond from the chaotic space in which it is forced to exist. In *The Bluest Eye*, as we have seen, the consequences of Pauline's denial of her daughter are exacerbated by her love for the white children in her charge. Sula's estrangement from her mother in Morrison's second novel and from her grandmother is at least partly responsible for her disregard of traditional wisdom normally passed down in African culture from the mother and for the way in which she fails to achieve a harmonious relationship with the other women in Medallion apart from Nel. Yet as Barbara Christian argues, it is through their reflections on this precarious role that the female slaves in *Beloved* are able to try to understand themselves as women and the concept often proves crucial to the survival of the self (Braxton and McLaughlin, 1990, 338–9). The effects of slavery on black women enable Morrison to pursue the consequences of the destruction of the mother–child bond on female identity further than she had in her earlier novels.

V

Beloved is not only a novel with a patchwork quilt structure which the reader has to piece together, but a text which literally demonstrates how any narrative has the potential to conceal a myriad of other narratives and how in emphasising one we often allow others to lie dormant and temporarily forgotten. The whites in this novel, for example, are anchored in texts which we need to recall if we are to understand slavery. Schoolteacher, for example, who makes a study of Sethe, is emblematic of a much larger text, the discourses around the pseudo-science of hierarchies expounded by scientists such as Herbert Spencer and Francis Galton. They came to rely upon colonial anthropology and vulgar interpretations of Darwinism to give coherence and respectability to popularly held racist myths. As Barbara Christian points out, schoolteacher's equivalents did write treatises on slaves based on scientific observation of them and measurement of various parts of their bodies (Braxton and McLaughlin, 1990, 338).

One of the most damning weapons of white, colonial power structures was the representation and stigmatising of Africans and African-Americans as beasts. This is a stereotype which *Beloved* specifically inverts whilst exposing it as the product of white cultural hegemony:

> White people believed that whatever the manners, under every dark skin was a jungle. Swift unnavigable waters, swinging screaming baboons, sleeping snakes, red gums ready for their sweet white blood . . . But it wasn't the jungle blacks brought with them to this place from the other (livable) place. It was the jungle whitefolks planted in them. And it grew. It spread. In, through and after life, it spread, until it invaded the whites who had made it. Touched them every one. Changed and altered them. Made them bloody, silly,

worse than even they wanted to be, so scared were they of the jungle they had made. The screaming baboon lived under their own white skin; the red gums were their own. (198–9)

The passage begins with an account of how whites have seen blacks which subtly encapsulates the narratives which have underpinned these views. These include the discovery and exploitation of foreign countries; the inability to appreciate the otherness of other cultures; and the fear of these cultures which caused whites to construct a blackness that said more about their concept of whiteness than the other races. Then these narratives are inverted. The constructions imposed by whites on black people are said to have compacted on themselves and in the potted narrative that follows we see how white ethnocentricity contains the seeds of its own destruction.

Amy, the white girl who helps Sethe to escape, introduces another subtext about slavery which has often been ignored and which develops Morrison's concern with the capitalist origins of the slave trade. The slavery endured by poor, working-class whites involved treatment at the hands of their masters which, as Sethe discovers, was not so dissimilar from her own. Indeed as Mbalia (1991) points out, denied education like the black slaves, Amy speaks in a similar vernacular: 'Be so pretty on me' and 'Mr Buddy whipped my tail' (95). The introduction of Amy also reminds us that non-European slaves were sought because their skin colour prevented them from blending, if they escaped, with the majority population. Similarly the Cherokee Indians who befriend runaway slaves remind us how the Indians were also taken as slaves and how the death of so many, through, for example, European disease, was one of the motivating factors behind the introduction of slaves from Africa and the West Indies.

One of the most powerful texts in the book is formed by Sethe's scars. Her own reading of them, since she has never actually seen them, is virtually a rememory of Amy's reading of them:

'Whitegirl. That's what she called it. I've never seen it and never will. But that's what she said it looked like. A chokecherry tree. Trunk, branches, and even leaves. Tiny little chokecherry leaves . . .' 16)

Characteristically of *Beloved*, there are different texts on Sethe's back. Amy's reading imaginatively transforms the pain and humiliation of

slavery. Later Sethe does the same in remembering the hanging of the
Sweet Home boys: 'Boys hanging from the most beautiful sycamores in
the world. It shamed her – remembering the wonderful soughing trees
rather than the boys' (6). When Sethe and Paul D first make love –
unsuccessfully because they are both burdened by their unresolved
pasts, symbolised by the clothes which they do not entirely remove –
Paul sees the scars differently from Amy and Sethe. Indeed he sees
them differently from when they began to make love; now they become
only 'a revolting clump of scars' (22). Paul D's inability to reclaim
Amy's text signifies the distance he and Sethe have yet to travel. Their
unsuccessful lovemaking and the issues involved are revisited obliquely
later in the text in the account of the two turtles mating. The male
turtle mounts the female from behind, reminding us of how Paul
approached Sethe at the stove. The female has to stretch out her neck
to touch the male's face, risking everything like Sethe coming out from
her protective shell of forgetting in making love with Paul. The shells of
the turtles clash as the pasts which Sethe and Paul bring with them and
with which they have to come to terms also conflict. The apparently
trivial incident of the two turtles becomes a visual text which acts as a
commentary upon a key event in the book. Lest we fail to give this
seemingly unimportant occurrence due consideration the text refers us
back to it when Beloved as incarnated ghost, apparently bent on
revenge against Sethe, seduces Paul D with her back to him, hoisting
her skirts and turning her head 'over her shoulder the way the turtles
had' (116). At this point in the novel the description of the landscape,
read emblematically, provides a further narrative and the context for
Beloved's death which she and others have to understand. The account
of the seasons – 'Each one enters like a prima donna, convinced its
performance is the reason the world has people in it' (116) – reminds us
of the white ethnocentricity which underpinned much of the African
slave trade. Autumn has 'bottles of blood and gold', encapsulating the
motivation, the greed and the consequences of slavery, whilst Paul D
hears the end of slavery, the end of white supremacy: 'the voices of
a dying landscape were insistent and loud' (116).

Beloved also provides us with subjects which few black writers had felt
themselves able to tackle, such as divisions within the black community
and the complicity between certain blacks and their white slave
owners. The neighbours who attend Baby Suggs' feast are the very
people who, the following day, are so envious of her position in the
community and her comparative affluence that they either remain

silent when the suspicious white strangers arrive or actually betray
Sethe. In an interview with Paul Gilroy (1993), Morrison finds a text in
the Garner story which had not previously been realised:

> It occurred to me that the questions about community and
> individuality were certainly inherent in that incident as I imagined
> it. When you are the community, when you are your children, when
> that is your individuality, there is no division . . . Margaret Garner
> didn't do what Medea did and kill her children because of some guy.
> It was for me this classic example of a person determined to be
> responsible. (177)

The significance of this concern with issues of community can only be
understood within the context of the betrayal of Baby Suggs. Indeed it
is in relation to Morrison's reading of the Mary Garner story that we
come to understand the chaos and disunity of the many sections of the
novel in which Beloved appears. Passages are left unpunctuated and
Beloved herself uses words out of order while omitting words important
to the sense all together: for example, 'Where your diamonds?'; 'Tell
me your earrings'. She frequently gets concepts wrong: 'Your woman
she never fix up your hair?' As Sethe's puzzled reaction suggests – 'My
woman? You mean my mother?' – Beloved has got hold of the wrong
text. The incoherence and chaos of the sections involving Beloved,
which at one point become poetry, are manifestations of the disunity
and isolation which she represents.

In African society moral judgement is invariably a matter for the
community to which the individual is answerable. In *Beloved* the
community which initially betrays Sethe significantly comes together at
the end of the novel and rescues her from killing Edward Bodwin.
Indeed Paul D's sudden reappearance after 18 years seems to cast him
as a representative of the community which judged her for what she
had done and which has to be reconvened as the only means by which
she can achieve full absolution. They, too, of course, can only achieve
absolution for betraying Baby Suggs and Sethe by coming together and
rescuing her. Although at one level the fragmentary structure of the
novel reflects the disunity of recent African-American history and the
chaos which slavery created in the lives of black people, at another level
it reflects the deeper structure in the black experience. The way in
which the novel moves without warning from the present in which it is
set to the past, denies the conventional division of the present, past and

future into separate units. The black experience is seen as a continuum, as a cycle which returns to the shared suffering which should consolidate the black community. This is the Word to which Hi Man refers and of which Baby Suggs speaks. In a sense, then, the sermon which Baby Suggs preaches in the clearing, which in the novel is itself emblematic of a homogeneous black community, is the really important text which lies buried in this novel. Indeed *Beloved* is ultimately about the recovery of this lost text.

This is the narrative which Geraldine in *The Bluest Eye* and Jadine in *Tar Baby*, for example, need to reclaim, for pursuing a single-minded version of success based on standardised white definitions of beauty, they deny their black cultural identity through shame and self-hatred. Geraldine, especially, epitomises the kind of self-interest which, in *Beloved*, divides the black community and causes its members to betray Baby Suggs. None of the narratives in *Beloved*, however, can be read independently of another, as the image of the quilt suggests. The integration of the different narratives within the novel is one of the keys to the healing process which it commends. This is evident from Paul D's return to Sethe at the end of the book; he sits rocking beside Sethe, a movement signifying healing and giving comfort, his eyes falling on the quilt which, like the novel, is more than the sum of its parts. The characters who achieve release in the novel do so through reclaiming or claiming narratives beyond those in which they have been locked.

Although the novel is set in the nineteenth century it has numerous implications for both black and white cultural identity in the twentieth century, as we intimated at the outset. These include the need for contemporary America to reclaim the full narrative of slavery, especially the suffering of black women; the need for white America to understand how slavery was justified as an intellectual and scientific project which failed to recognise the human cost; and the need for white culture to appreciate that the brutality and racialism of slavery has extended far beyond the emancipation of slaves in the nineteenth century into the late twentieth century.

Morrison herself saw the African-American novel as a healing art form:

> For a long time, the art form that was healing for Black people was music. That music is no longer exclusively ours; we don't have exclusive rights to it. Other people sing it and play it; it is the mode of contemporary music everywhere. So another form has to take that

place, and it seems to me that the novel is needed by African-Americans in a way that it was not needed before . . . (Morrison in Evans, 1984, 340)

Healing is at the centre of *Beloved* and is centred on Sethe as Amy, Baby Suggs and, finally, Paul D contribute to her healing process. Baby Suggs' message is also one of healing by learning to value oneself and to join with other black people. Almost the final thing Paul D remembers in the novel is Sixo describing Thirty-Mile Woman: 'She is a friend of mind. She gather me, man. The pieces I am in, she gather them and give them back to me in all the right order' (272–3). But the novel does not exorcise the enormity of the fracture which slavery and white racism have created – although it concludes on a note of healing, there is no definitive sense of closure. At the most basic level of the story we do not know how completely Sethe will be healed or whether she and Paul D have been sufficiently successful in exorcising their respective pasts to be able to make a life together. Their particular narrative ends with Sethe's incredulity – 'Me? Me?' – while the novel concludes with a pain and loneliness that's 'an inside kind – wrapped tight like skin . . . No rocking can hold it down' (274).

7

Jazz (1992)

Jazz is set in Harlem during 'The Harlem Renaissance', in 1926, midway through a decade when the United States was in the throes of 'The Jazz Age' or 'The Roaring Twenties'. White histories of the period tend to see its creative and cultural ferment as a response to the Armistice of 1919. But Harlem and the city in general had a different significance for African-Americans and it is this, rather than the post-war euphoria which was essentially part of white history, which Morrison tries to recover in *Jazz*. In this respect, the focus of interest is the same as in the early novels; the black communities which exist behind and which transcend the boundaries drawn up by the whites to define and contain them.

On one level Harlem's significance derives from black migration, itself a response to the 'want and violence' (33) of reconstruction, one of the narratives in black history which, as we said in the previous chapter, is reclaimed in *Beloved*. A fundamental and irreversible shift took place during the half century after the Civil War; initially the Southern cities drew large numbers of ex-slaves from their hinterlands, but the segregation, the violence and the poverty drove hundreds of thousands of African-Americans northwards. But if this narrative had to be reclaimed for the African-American novel, it was already preserved in the blues which articulated for generations of black people the aspirations, difficulties and frustrations of their transition not only from slavery, but from a rural to an urban lifestyle.

The city generally assumed legendary significance in African-American mythology through stories told, for example, by porters and waiters working on Pullman trains or through letters sent from friends

112

and relatives. In the Northern cities blacks could make their own decisions, including whom to love, although they rarely enjoyed the unbridled liberties of the mythology; they could enjoy higher wages, though never as high as the stories which circulated in the South would have them believe. But whatever the discrepancies between the dream and the reality, there were significant new-found freedoms and excitements. The language used in the South to describe the cities of the North actually took on the same biblical connotations – The Promised Land, Canaan – as during the period of slavery. Harlem's own legendary status is encapsulated in *Jazz* in the narrator's initial description of it, related from the point of view of the incoming migrants who are said to fall in love with it unequivocally and 'forever'. The description in fact echoes accounts of Harlem at the time from writers such as Langston Hughes, who wrote on his arrival:

I can never put on paper the thrill of the underground ride to Harlem . . . At every station I kept watching for the sign; 135th Street . . . I went up the steps and out into the bright September sunlight. Harlem! I stood there, dropped my bags, took a deep breath and felt happy again. (1986, 81)

For Hughes, Harlem is a place where he can breathe again and rediscover himself. At one point the City in Morrison's novel has no air, only 'breath'. In *Jazz*, the City allows people to be themselves; 'their stronger, riskier selves' (33).

The city as a subject was approached more tentatively in *Tar Baby* where, as we have seen, Jadine's enthusiasm for the opportunities that it provided for black women stands in contradistinction to Son's initial impressions of New York. Son's view of the city is redolent of those voices of the twenties disillusioned with metropolitan life; like writers such as T. S. Eliot, Son stresses a social and moral malaise. But Son provides a specifically black slant: the men are accused of having eschewed their black identity and the women are said to be crying beneath their plum lipstick. *Jazz*, however, like black writing on Harlem in the twenties, stresses the way in which the city allows black people to be 'more like themselves'. Whilst Son in *Tar Baby* searches in vain for elderly black people and black children on the streets of New York, Harlem in the twenties is a different kind of place packed with black children, young girls, men, mothers and 'barfly women'.

II

Although *Jazz* is indebted to the aesthetics of African-American music, Morrison admitted in an interview that the title might not be right for the novel, believing jazz itself to be more in the background of the book as image and metaphor (Bigsby, 1992). Despite her reservations, the influence of jazz where the melody is introduced and then subsequently unravelled and embellished, is clear from the outset where the essence of the story is unfurled within the first ten lines and then subsequently retold from different viewpoints. In jazz, as Rice (1992) points out, musicians play against each other, each establishing a unique sound in the ensemble which is sometimes developed in long solo pieces. In the novel, various characters relate their versions of what has happened, mirroring 'the group nature of jazz music, exemplifying how a singular art work is constructed from several solo voices'. There is an improvised quality to the book, even by the standards of Morrison's previous novels, in its use of time and ellipses, as well as in the way the narrator frequently hands over to different voices. The light, airy music of ragtime, to which jazz is partly indebted, was an attempt to capture the mood of the decade which the novel in places also tries to recreate in its prose style. But there was a heavier, melancholy strain to the decade and to jazz itself which we also find as a counterpoint to the optimism in Morrison's novel and evident even from a cursory summary of the plot. For amongst those who have 'train danced' to the city from the South are Violet and Joe Trace. Joe has murdered his young lover, Dorcas, who has been unfaithful to him and to whom he was initially attracted by the inattentions of his wife who had taken to sleeping with a doll because she could not have children. Since all this is revealed early in the novel, its focus is upon the consequences of the murder for Joe and Violet. At the outset of the book, Violet, who becomes known in the community as Violent, driven by jealousy, tries to mutilate Dorcas' corpse at the funeral. Fortunately for her, Dorcas' guardian, Alice, refuses to disclose the name of her ward or the name of the person who tries to mutilate her body.

Jazz, however, provides only one of many contributory strands to this novel. Cautioned by Morrison's own scepticism about the appropriateness of the title, we should resist trying to discover a singular source for her aesthetics especially given the development of her experimental, multi-vocal narratives over more than two decades.

Jazz, like *The Bluest Eye* and *Song of Solomon,* moves backwards and forwards in time. Like *Song of Solomon,* it takes us on a reverse journey from that which many black Americans undertook after the Civil War; the novel in retracing the past lives of Joe, Violet and their families takes the reader from the North to the South, from the city to the country, and from the twentieth to the nineteenth century. In doing so it provides the reader with vivid glimpses of the South after emancipation. Indeed the impact of the previous century is more significant in *Jazz* than in *Song of Solomon,* underscoring the importance upon it of *Beloved.* In an interview (Bigsby, 1992), Morrison argues that *Beloved* was 'necessary' to the writing of *Jazz*: 'I would not have understood what the later period was without knowing what it reacted against'. For Morrison, '*Jazz* is about the release of love' and she believes: 'It wouldn't have had the force it did, had I not realised the threat which love posed during slavery and reconstruction'.

Morrison has suggested that the book is 'a jazz gesture' which draws on what jazz says about the people of the time and about the sensual way in which people related to one another (Bigsby, 1992). As Rodrigues (1993) observes: 'More than just a story of three individuals, the novel, a continuation of *Beloved,* jazzifies the history of a people' (742). Urban black music embraced the complexity of human relationships and the stresses placed on them, sometimes with anger and frustration but sometimes with melting sentimentality and all these emotions are played off against each other in Morrison's novel. The image of women in the Jazz Age was ambiguous; projected in the films of the time, which were essentially white, as light-hearted, unconventional and daring, but in song, where there was a much more obvious black presence, as melancholic, even tragic. As Shaw (1987) points out, there were numerous songs of unrequited love and of loss. Despair and resignation were keynotes of popular torch songs such as 'I'd Rather Be Blue over You (Than Be Happy with Somebody Else)', 'I Cried for You (Now It's Your Turn to Cry over Me)', and 'Day by Day You're Going to Miss Me' (78). The novel highlights the same concerns of the period as the music; loneliness, the changeability of feelings, emotional insecurity in personal relationships and the anguish of failure. In doing so, it draws on the personalised nature of jazz lyrics which enabled singers and songwriters, such as the one featured in the novel, to break new ground in exploring emotional situations. Taking its cue from jazz, the novel alternates between external description and internal longings such as Violet's desire to have a baby, which becomes 'heavier than sex: a panting, unmanageable craving' (180); the kind of loss suffered by Violet and also articulated in the novel by Alice; and the jealous thirst for vengeance experienced by a number of the novel's characters. Indeed it is the sensuality, the unpredictability and the dissonance of African-American life during the Jazz Age which the novel probes and develops.

III

From Cholly's rape of Pecola in *The Bluest Eye* and Eva's rumoured amputation of her leg on a railway line in *Sula*, Morrison's texts have involved and have often revolved around a series of unpredictable, even ostensibly inexplicable, events. *Jazz* opens with an incident anchored in the kind of subjectivism which in her novels is never totally socialised. But Violet's interruption of Dorcas' funeral service is only one of the acts for which she is well known, others include the occasion when she suddenly sat down in the street. Such incidents challenge the routinised behaviours of others by which everyday reality is maintained. When the funeral episode is revisited later in the novel, the emphasis is placed upon the ushers who have to eschew the respect for their elders with which they have been brought up in order to remove her.

It is not only Violet's eccentric behaviour – ex-centric in the sense that it is marginal to the routinised and centred patterns of social behaviour – which serves to focus the unpredictable in this novel. Joe's falling in love with Dorcas is also unexpected and his murder of her inexplicable. The first full-length description of his character is reminiscent of Paul D's personality in *Beloved*. Like Paul D, he is a man whom women trust, in whom they confide and with whom they establish something of the rapport usually reserved for other women. In *Jazz* the level of interest in the unpredictable is enhanced by the unreliability of the narrator whose identity is uncertain and whose grasp on the narrative is finally lost: 'The fact that the narrator of the book doesn't always know what happened is part of that conflict between imposed knowledge, fate, and a dissonance, an uncertainty, which is what makes life so original' (Bigsby, 1992). From the first time that we encounter one of the narrator's asides – 'Maybe she [Violet] thought she could solve the mystery of love that way. Good luck and let me know' (5) – we are made aware that she is a destabilising element in the narrative. Whilst overtly directing the reader's response, for example, in the description of Dorcas' aunt as hardheaded and sly, she admits that she is not the best judge of character; she has lived too long in her own mind, she hasn't mixed with people enough and she needs to get out more.

Some of the instability within the narrative also reflects the violence and criminality of the city to which it draws attention. The social space of the novel, where the instability of the urban meets the unpredictability of jazz, is especially volatile and Dorcas' association of the war with partying during the Jazz Age encapsulates the uncertainty and unpredictability of people's lives in the 1920s:

> In war or at a party everyone is wily, intriguing; goals are set and altered; alliances rearranged. Partners and rivals devastated; new pairings triumphant. (191)

All of Morrison's novels explore the geographical and the political. It is customary now to talk of a 'new geography' or a 'postmodern geography' because long-held positivist notions of space as static and autonomous have given way to an emphasis on space as the product of wider sociopolitical processes (Soja, 1989; Keith and Pile, 1993). As we have seen, the power of the propertied classes to change the geography of an area is a subject of concern in *The Bluest Eye* in the segregated Lake Shore Park, for example, and even more so in *Sula* where the prologue describes the redevelopment of a black neighbourhood in a small Ohio town by white propertied interests. But the 'new geography' provides an especially useful approach to *Jazz* which focuses on how African-American music in the 1920s, developed by both black and white musicians, was building a space which shaped and was shaped by people's behaviour and which in turn was influenced by this particular musical discourse. In this respect an important analogy is provided in the novel by the marchers in July 1917 who are 'moving slowly into the space the drums were building for them' (53). Many of the characters in *Jazz* similarly occupy a space which jazz is constructing for them, a space in which morality, life styles, familial patterns and religion are being renegotiated.

In the novel it is Alice who specifically identifies the role of African-American music in shaping the social space into which people are being drawn even though she fails to recognise that the music reflects the experiences of black people:

It was the music. The dirty, get-on-down music the women sang and
the men played and both danced to, close and shameless or apart
and wild . . . It made you do unwise disorderly things. Just hearing
it was like viòlating the law. (58)

Lawlessness was the flipside of life in the city in the twenties – the
narrator in *Jazz* alludes to ordinary people taking the law into their
own hands – but probably no more so than in any other period. The
twenties appeared wild and disorderly because, as Bradbury observes,
it was an era of new manners, of self-conscious fashions and of the
exploration of new tastes (Bradbury and Palmer, 1971, 12). The
narrator, enthusiastic about Harlem and excited by its people, becomes
increasingly aware of, and interested in, how this self-consciousness is
linked to violence as integral features of life in the Jazz Age. Even the
gangsters at one point are said to be aware that they are 'being watched
for excitement' (7). The 'hoodlums', as they were more affectionately
known, were idealised by the public despite the blood on their hands.
Prohibition was such an unpopular law in the United States that the
agents who tried to enforce it found themselves cast as the real villains
of the twenties while the bootleggers, the speakeasy owners, the rum
runners and the hijackers became, as the narrator in the'novel suggests,
hoodlums 'handing out goodies'. In the first image that we have of the
City, its buildings are being cut in half by daylight as if by a razor; a
metaphor that keeps Violet's attempt to slash the face of Dorcas' corpse
to the fore whilst anticipating the generalised violence of the
metropolis. But the most important function of the first image of the
City is to emphasise the 'looking faces' where it is difficult if not
impossible to distinguish between those of the inhabitants and those
carved by stonemasons. According to the narrator, survival depends
upon being streetwise, a key element of which is learning to 'watch
everything and everyone and try to figure out their plans, their
reasonings, long before they do' (8).

IV

The Jazz Age was the decade which saw the motion picture industry
come into its own and by 1926 there were over 20,000 cinemas in
America. The influence of the movies in *Jazz* is different from in *The*

Bluest Eye where the emphasis is on its representation of white, middle-class American values and standards of beauty. In *Jazz* the stress falls on the preoccupation with visual images in a culture where visual impact is given priority over other sensual impressions. But *Jazz* returns to subjects raised in the first book, the loss of sensuality and the separation of the 'internal' and the 'external'. The cinema is the most 'imaginary' of art forms in which representation is the most enigmatic, the farthest removed from the recording of an authentic experience. The distance between image and reality is a key motif in *Jazz*. Dorcas, for example, is accused by the narrator of regarding everything as if it were a picture show evidenced in her obliviousness to the fact that Joe is a married man, much older than herself and very restricted in the amount of time he can spend with her. The difference between the image which she has of them as a couple and the reality is especially obvious when she raises with Joe the possibility of them escaping for a while to Mexico. But other characters, too, seem to occupy space as imaginary as the image on the cinema screen; for example, Joe's own association of Dorcas with a piece of sweet candy and Violet taking dolls to bed. Others, too, have been influenced by the new emphasis of the age on visual consumption where people are cast increasingly into the role of voyeur. The split which theorists such as Julia Kristeva and Jacques Lacan have identified between the 'I' who speaks and the 'I' who is spoken becomes increasingly pronounced in the novel. What worries Felice about the time when she and Dorcas made up love scenes and described them to each other is the picture which she had of herself doing it. Violet perceives each of the public events in which she behaves eccentrically as 'scenes'; she does not see herself doing them but sees them being done. Both the 'scenes' described in the novel involve a violation of conventions attached to observation. Violet in attacking Dorcas' face violates the custom of 'viewing' the corpse whilst in stealing the baby she reneges on the trust implicit in being asked to 'watch' a child for its mother. Watching, being watched and looking in mirrors are, in fact, salient motifs in the novel: Violet's birdcages have mirrors where the birds can watch themselves; Dorcas practises in front of the mirror to tell Joe that she wishes to end their relationship; and Joe needs a mirror to see the pictures which Dorcas has drawn on his body with lipstick. As Rigney (1990) suggests in a discussion of Hagar in *Song of Solomon*, mirrors are dangerous objects in Morrison's fiction because of the vision of self that they reflect, representing white standards of beauty or the illusion of a unified self. In *Jazz*, they mark a transition from one social reality to another but one where what is reflected represents a greater regression from black social norms.

One of the indicators of this regression is the way in which the 'inner' and the 'outer' become increasingly separated, as we suggested briefly above. The separation of the external and the internal is part of the experience of seeing oneself in a mirror for it allows us to see ourselves both as self and as other. Mirrors provide an objective perspective on what is otherwise a subjective aspect. According to Felice, Joe has 'double eyes', each of a different colour, one that enables the observer to look into him and another which allows Joe to look into the observer. They are emblematic of a kind of schizophrenia which develops within him. Eventually discovering that he is only able to recall a visual narrative of his life with Violet, he is unable to reclaim how he felt with her. After killing Dorcas, he panics when the visual memories of her begin to fade as if without them there is nothing. This separation of the external person from feeling and emotion pervades the Jazz Age. Dorcas seems to live apart from her body as if it is something that is worn by the self. One night at the age of 16, she is said to have 'stood in her body' whilst she and Felice 'come to know that a badly dressed body is nobody at all' (65). The knowledge referred to here is not a universal truth, if indeed any do exist, but a tuning into the culture of the decade. Dorcas and Felice come to realise that whilst mirrors reflect back to women their fascination with their own image, it is a fascination dominated, as Coward (1985) maintains, with discontent; every woman's mirror image is disturbed by the critical glance of the cultural ideal (80). Morrison's pun on 'nobody' emphasises how people in the Jazz Age are judged on external appearance; the brothers who attract attention at the party which Dorcas and Felice attend know this, and have smiles which function like light bulbs. It is a ruthless subculture; especially for women who as objects of the male gaze are judged by men on the basis of the visual impression they make. Dorcas, 'the peppermint girl with the bad skin' (69), finds herself 'acknowledged, appraised and dismissed in the time it takes for a needle to find its opening groove'. As Coward (1985) points out, 'the ability to scrutinise is premised on power' (75). Women's inability to return such a critical look is a sign of subordination; often averting the eyes then risking, as Coward says, male attention turning into aggression. One of the scenarios played out before the narrator in her early description of the City involves a meeting between a man and a woman. Although we, like the narrator, know nothing about them, it is clear that we are watching a display in power relationships. All the actions confirm that the power lies with the man; he silences the woman's earnest conversation (we do not know what it is about) by touching her lips; he is able to tilt her head which causes her to relax and to loosen her grip on her purse; he places his hands on the wall so that she is below them. As readers we have no knowledge of what is being said; it is like watching a silent movie. But the body language would seem to suggest that a woman is judged attractive to the male when she conforms to his expectations of her behaviour, particularly sexual behaviour.

Surveillance of the space created by the African-American music and of the streets is converted in the subculture of the twenties into the pleasure of being watched: at a party, a mere touch is enough to lift one's spirit to the ceiling 'where it floats for a bit looking down with pleasure on the dressed-up nakedness below' (188). But this pleasure in being watched is both a reflection of the preoccupation of the age with the visual and part of the emancipatory spirit of the decade. As Shaw (1987) points out, the Nineteenth Constitutional Amendment, passed on 28 August 1920, which gave women the right to vote, significantly affected the mood and mores of the 1920s (12). It helped turn it into a radical decade as far as behaviour and consciousness were concerned; characterised by an emancipated sexual mores, an increasingly accelerated and tense pace of life and an enormous shift in the moral focus. Jazz and the blues articulated a cultural and political struggle over sexual relations directed at reclaiming women's sexuality and their bodies from the objectification of female sexuality within a patriarchal order. But jazz and the blues were only partly responsible for creating the culture of the 1920s. The films of the time also appeared to celebrate the new woman and the new morality, although they often ended with the 'flappers' and 'It' girls marrying into middle-class respectability. They carried titles such as *Forbidden Fruit, Flapper Wives, Weekend Wives, Bedroom and Bath, Madness of Youth, Children of Divorce, Modern Maidens* and *Dancing Mothers*. Advertisements for them spoke of 'Brilliant men, beautiful jazz babies, champagne baths, midnight revels, petting parties in the purple dawn, all ending in one terrific smashing climax that makes you gasp' (Bradbury and Palmer, 1971, 51). The new spirit is perhaps best indicated in a quotation from Zelda Fitzgerald shortly before she left for Europe in 1924:

I'm raising my girl to be a flapper. I like the jazz generation, and I hope my daughter's generation will be jazzier. I want my girl to do as she pleases . . . I think a woman gets more happiness out of being gay, light-hearted, unconventional, mistress of her own fate, than out of a career that calls for hard work, intellectual pessimism and loneliness. I don't want Pat to be a genius. I want her to be a flapper, because flappers are brave and gay and beautiful. (Milford, 1971, 160)

Jazz is located firmly in black Harlem, however, and the wider, essentially white world of the 'flappers', which was the focus of work by white writers such as F. Scott Fitzgerald, only enters the novel indirectly. Yet, as we shall see, it is to this kind of morality that the narrator's own attempt at an improvised piece on love is intended as a counterpoint.

The women included in the initial description of the City in *Jazz* are located in the space between the objectification of women within the male gaze and the reclamation of their bodies and their sexuality as sites of their own subjectivity:

The woman who churned a man's blood as she leaned all alone on a fence by a country road might not expect even to catch his eye in the City. But if she is clipping quickly down the big-city street in heels, swinging her purse, or sitting on a stoop with a cool beer in her hand, dangling her shoe from the toes of her foot, the man, reacting to her posture, to soft skin on stone, the weight of the building stressing the delicate, dangling shoe, is captured. And he'd think it was the woman he wanted, and not some combination of curved stone, and a swinging, high-heeled shoe moving in and out of sunlight. (34)

Here the reader's attention is drawn to what mediates these images. The socially constructed space which the women have come to occupy according to a socially recognised style of behaviour is emphasised more than the women themselves. For the women remain anonymous types rather than individuals. But what is also depicted is the man's status as spectator, his relation to the body images which serve as a means of articulating identity and difference, even of challenging boundaries. As often in the visually dominated culture of the twentieth century, images of women reflect the obsessive distancing of them.

Individual gestures are signs that acquire meaning from the subculture which they signify. The verb 'clipping' emphasises the woman's self-confident sexuality and the way she walks so as to centre herself in the male gaze, reinforcing the high heels themselves as one of Western culture's most potent sexual symbols. Her swinging purse signifies a daring abandonment which calls attention to herself and to what women in a city with a great deal of crime might otherwise wish to conceal. The other woman also appears to be at the centre of a socially constructed space which allows her to construct an identity, albeit with a masculinised bias, that signifies devil-may-care self-confidence. A woman drinking beer in public in the 1920s signified the subversion of traditional notions of femininity and conventional modes of behaviour; a recalcitrance which epitomised the Jazz Age itself. Again the high-heeled shoe is significant; in itself suggesting sexuality, but swinging from the woman's foot conveying a sense of unfettered, sexual confidence which the man who is cast as a voyeur finds – and is meant to find – seductive, at least at a distance.

Shaw (1987) attributes many of the changes in what was socially acceptable behaviour for women to the Nineteenth Constitutional Amendment including 'women smoking in public, bobbing their hair (to look more like men), seductively raising the hem of their skirts, rolling their stockings to expose bare knees, and flaunting their sexuality' (12). But all this was encouraged, as he observes, by the music of the decade. Alice's memories in *Jazz* of how her parents brought her up is indirectly an assessment of how far conventions had changed in the twenties. Alice's upbringing is also intended as an explanation for the repressive attitudes which she passed on to Dorcas and may be one of the reasons why Dorcas turned out as she did. But Alice provides a commentary on the repression which the 1920s removed for women. She remembers being instructed that there was a 'womanish' way to sit, with legs crossed, warned about slumping at table and told firmly about 'switching' when she walked. As soon as her breasts developed they were 'bound and resented' while her legs were always hidden, her parents frowned when they could not lower the hems any further. In the style of jazz composition, Alice's memories embellish the narrator's description of the women discussed above and act as a counterpoint to them. However, the contrast is not simply a matter of changing fashions. The women who clip down steps in high heels swinging their purses and who drink beer in public exude a new-found confidence and pride in themselves and their sexuality. As a counterpoint to Joe's observations on the easy availability of some of the women, Alice respects women who have not surrendered to male expectations, especially those who protect themselves with violence. Her memory of the Swedish tailor for whom she worked telling her of the negress who slashed his face from ear to mouth and her memories of other men with facial injuries articulate the depth of the change that was taking place. For behind these stories of men getting their comeuppance there are untold narratives of sexual harassment, of black women being fondled in kitchens, called names and even being punched in the face by police. Once again in the style of jazz composition, Alice revisits an earlier statement by the narrator, embellishing it and approaching it from a different angle. Her ruminations on the folded blades which some black women carried, their packets of lye and the shards of glass which they taped to their hands provide a commentary on the narrator's earlier insistence on the need to be streetwise, to watch people and try to figure out what they are going to do before they know themselves.

Dorcas herself epitomises the interconnection between the recalcitrant nature of the decade and its music; how social and sexual boundaries were being challenged; and the increased emphasis upon the importance of being in the social gaze. She never allows herself, nor is ever allowed, to come into her own existence because those who are drawn to her eventually reject her or are rejected by her. Her men friends are generally frightened off, not only because she encourages them to break the law but because she gives them the impression that there is no inner consistency to her. For her everything seems to be a kaleidoscope of actions and reactions with little beyond; everything appears to be like 'a picture show'. It is significant that she has to practise her leaving speech to Joe in a mirror because in her world nothing is stable enough or meaningful enough to permit vital linguistic communication to begin. Although there is quite a lot of social and sexual contact, there is no inter-subjectivity; she comes to enjoy occupying the gaze of others. When she is with Acton at the party in which she is killed, for example, she touches him not for her own pleasure but because she knows that other girls in the room are watching her enviously. He appears to have a magnetic power over others as if by being drawn to him women will fill the gap in their lives. But the emotional space in which Dorcas finds herself is confusing and conflictual, located between the demands of Acton and the undemanding gaze of Joe. In setting their contradictory expectations and views of her in opposition to each other, Dorcas imitates the structural nature of jazz.

Having become increasingly an object of other people's gazes, it is appropriate that Dorcas becomes a spectator of her own death. One of the first things she notices is that heads are turning to watch her fall while the superficiality of constantly occupying spaces constructed by the gaze of others is betrayed by Acton's response to her; he is more concerned about the blood on his jacket and shirt. As the recurring mirror images throughout the novel suggest, surface is more important than substance. Dorcas eventually occupies, if only she would realise it, a world given over to surfaces, outlines and veils. Indeed Dorcas herself is less worried by the prospect of death than by missing something important which she senses is about to happen.

V

The motifs of watching and being watched are central to the novel's pursuit of the subject of obsession, a theme developed from *Beloved* and pursued in *Jazz* on a number of different levels. Whilst Colonel Wordsworth Gray's rage at the fact that his daughter is pregnant by a black boy, Hunters Hunter, expresses itself in a violent slap, the repulsion in the look which her mother gives her has the greater and more lasting impact. As throughout Morrison's work, the body is the visible representation of the identity by which black people are victimised. When Vera Louise and her black maid, True Belle, bath her son, he is conscious of, but does not understand, the looks that pass between them as they examine the backs of his hands and his hair. At another level Violet's longing for a child, which is described as a 'deep-dreaming' in which she is drowning, finds expression in obsessively staring at infants and toy displays at Christmas. But it is Dorcas who is the object of the key fixations with which the novel is concerned. Joe and Violet in their obsession with her are united yet distinguished one from another in their shared fixation with her photograph staring from their mantelpiece. In describing Joe's behaviour after he has killed Dorcas, how he thinks about her all the time and how he cannot work or sleep, Violet is really describing in so many words her own preoccupation with the young woman. As intensely as Dorcas appears to stare out of the photograph at Violet, Violet studies the detail of Dorcas' gaze, even noticing that her split ends need trimming. Each of them sees different things in Dorcas' gaze: whilst for Joe her face exudes calm and generosity, for Violet her stare is haughty and greedy.

Violet's obsession with Dorcas is realised in her search to discover everything she can about her, but Joe's obsession reaches its climax in his journey to kill her.

At their most obsessive, both Joe and Violet confirm the narrator's observation early in the novel that if you do not know when to love and when to quit you end up being controlled by a force outside yourself. The extent to which Joe is in the grip of his obsession when he sets out to murder Dorcas is conveyed in the way his consciousness appears to collapse in retreat from the seeming unreality around him. As he journeys with his gun into the City to find her, he is driven at a deep level by a primitive instinct which emerges while his moral being lapses into amnesia. Obviously something is gained by this return to the mindless drives of a primitive, instinctual being, but the narrative emphasises what is lost. His speechless, physical contact with the other passengers in the railway carriage, such as the woman who returns the bag in which his gun is concealed, is emblematic of the way he is regressing from the world around him. Increasingly, he moves unconsciously in the space between his past and his present and the different levels which compose social reality. His observation, as mediated by the narrator, of the girls who 'clack' down the stairs from the train and his noticing their red lips and their stockinged legs that appear to 'whisper' to each other suggests how he now sees himself surrounded by mere mechanical fabrications of the social system. The kinds of signs which the narrator sees in the City women whom we discussed above, acquiring meaning from the subculture in which they are based, are now seen by Joe as agents in the exchange of themselves. Up to a point, the make-up and stockings are signs of the power which they have accrued in reclaiming their bodies and their sexuality as part of their own subjectivity. But they are now seen, in Joe's eyes, surrendering this power to the male right to overcome and penetrate them.

In the style of jazz composition, the novel concludes with the narrator attempting an improvisory piece on the quality of mature love which acts as a counterpoint to the relationship between Joe and Dorcas. Dorcas, as we have said, emphasised the body as something to be seen. Trying to persuade Joe to take her to Mexico, she worries him by suggesting that they can sit at round tables with lamps on them. The final improvisation on love is introduced by a passage which recommends that the body is 'the vehicle' not 'the point' of love; whereas Dorcas stresses the visual, the narrator here emphasises touch.

Indeed the concluding section of the novel subverts all the earlier insistence on watching and being watched: 'They are under the covers because they don't have to look at themselves any more; there is no stud's eye, no chippie glance to undo them' (228). The 'whispers' between longtime lovers under the covers contrast with, and are a commentary upon, Dorcas' aspiration that she and Joe will be able to spend their time touching each other intimately in secret beneath the tablecloths in Mexico. Whereas many of the characters in the novel are concerned with looking out into the various gazes upon them, these older lovers are perceived as being turned inwards towards each other.

In the final page of the novel, the narrator reveals herself as someone who has experienced only the kind of secret affairs promoted in the films and the advertising which constructed the independently-minded and rebellious 'flapper'. But she envies the way in which legitimate lovers are able to express their feelings in public by touching each other across a table and straightening or brushing each other's clothes. Her own improvisation on love celebrates monogamy and faithfulness; a counterpoint to the so-called new morality of the Jazz Age. Conversely much of the novel, the difficulties, anguish and frustrations of love in the twenties, acts as a counterpoint to this final piece – as we would expect in a jazz composition.

Jazz then is a novel which is not so much about the music but the lives of the people during the decade which the music helped to create. Although jazz obviously influenced the structure and style of the novel, it would be rather limiting not to see the book in the way in which we have approached all of Morrison's novels in this study. Like her other works, *Jazz* is concerned with aspects of African-American history and experience which had not previously been articulated. Its experiments with form and language are derived not only from jazz as a form of music but also from its radical content.

8

The Language

I want to show the beauty of our language, its rhythms, its metaphors, its poetry. Our people speak beautifully, with the rhythms of the Bible, of sermons. But they were told they could not speak, which is often how cultures are marginalised. (Morrison in Kenyon, 1993, 18)

We come to literature for the experience of the language as much as for the abstract ideas and philosophies. If we are not arrested, challenged or made to marvel by an author's language then it is unlikely we will establish a rapport with a text. Throughout this study, we have drawn attention to the multi-layered nature of Morrison's work, especially the ways in which it is indebted to African, European and biblical myths. It has been impossible in a discussion of her work to ignore its preoccupation with the processes of labelling and naming as the functioning of the Symbolic Order: for example, the ironic allocation of the name 'Peace' to the family whose members disrupt the black community of Medallion; the highly significant names given to some of the geographical locations, such as the 'Bottoms', or to individuals, such as Macon Dead, Milkman, Son or Pilate. The multi-layered composition of the texts is evident in the polyphonous nature of the way events are conceived. The imagery describing the bargeman's retrieval of Chicken Little from the water in *The Bluest Eye* is a case in point. It employs verbs – 'netted' and 'hauled' – which cast the bargeman in the role of a fisherman, maybe even associating him with Christ, the fisher of men. But this imagery stands in contradistinction to how the corpse, the body of a black boy, is 'dumped' in a burlap sack and 'tossed' among empty egg crates. The empty crates not only emphasise the waste of a young life but, together with the indifference, if not contempt, with which the body is treated, undermine the spiritual connotations of the activity of fishing. Yet even analysing the different levels of meaning and significance in the works still leaves much to be said about the quality of their prose. At their best Morrison's novels mine rich, linguistic seams that are easily the equal of the hitherto unspoken narratives, the deep secret thoughts and, sometimes, the terrible yearnings which have not been previously articulated in novel form.

There is insufficient space here to make more than a few key observations about Morrison's use of language. But one of the most noticeable features is the vividness of the writing, a characteristic of African-American English as even a cursory familiarity with jazz lyrics demonstrates. This could be illustrated from the novels by the description of the woman in yellow in *Tar Baby* who walks 'as though her many-coloured sandals were pressing gold tracks on the floor' (42). Or by some of the uncompromising observations of violence, metonymic of much larger canvases of horror; for example, the description of Shadrack in the trenches of the First World War seeing the running body of a headless soldier 'ignoring altogether the drip and slide of brain tissue down its back' (*Sula*, 8). But more characteristic of the works is the innovative articulation of what might otherwise be quite bland or clichéd from another author; for example, how Pilate in *Song of Solomon* on her arrival in Shalimar 'blended into the population like a stick of butter in a churn' (335). Or the description of the city sky in *Jazz*: 'It can go purple and keep an orange heart so the clothes of the people on the streets glow like dance-hall costumes' (36). Or the dark of the early evening which Cholly and Darlene hope to enjoy together: 'The sun had gone and pulled away its shreds of light' (*The Bluest Eye*, 114). Colours contribute much to the impact of Morrison's writing and often they are appreciated in a sensual and tactile rather than a purely visual way, as if it were possible to touch them as colours rather than touch coloured objects. This is suggested by the description of physical responses to them; for example, Cholly and Darlene are said to have 'sank down' in the green-and-purple grass where it is clear that what they sink into are the colours as much, if not more so, than the grass itself. Significantly all the characters in *Beloved*, the most colourless of the novels, search for colour, as Rigney points out (1990, 59). But although the vividness of her writing derives from the priority which Morrison gives to the senses without giving one priority over another, equally if not more important is the *jouissance* and fluidity of the prose, drawing on the rhythms and creativity of black speech.

Homi Bhabha (1994), drawing attention to the constitutive energies in plural societies, has observed that the dynamism of cultural difference lies in its metaphoric mode of enunciation and negotiation. This is evident in Morrison's work in what appears to be at times a kind of 'folk creativity', often employing metaphors derived from the animal and natural world. When Mrs MacTeer in *The Bluest Eye* breaks off a switch to discipline the children who are fighting she complains: 'I'd rather raise pigs than some nasty girls. Least I can slaughter *them*!' (22); Miss Marie accuses the sockless Pecola of being as 'bare-legged as a yard dog' (39). In *Jazz*, when Rose is evicted from her home, she is tipped from her chair 'the way you get the cat off the seat if you don't want to touch it . . .' (98). This folk creativity draws on a larger communal resource, in which personal and communal memories become fused, consisting of localised myths, stories, vignettes and anecdotes, possibly exaggerated over time. It can be most obviously illustrated with reference to *Sula* or the men in *Song of Solomon*: '[The people] had seen women pull their dresses over their heads and howl like dogs for lost love. And men who sat in doorways with pennies in their mouths for lost love' (128) As Trudier Harris points out, in general, Morrison's characters adhere to many folk beliefs, superstitions and signs common to historical communities (McKay, 1988, 69). *The Bluest Eye*, for example, virtually opens with Claudia's memory of her mother's treatment for colds. However, the linguistic richness of much of the writing stems from the realisation that communal memory is not accessed through the language but stored in it. Thus in *Sula*, the exasperation and the oppression of the hottest day of the year is in the imagery of cats splaying their fur like quills and hot flies sleeping (70). This communal memory enables the narrators of *The Bluest Eye* and of *Sula*, for example, to tap an imaginative and linguistic resource beyond what could be expected of their own vocabulary and personal recollections; to provide a level of linguistic innovation that does not overly strain their credibility. Indeed as Harris says, the metaphors distinguish between characters like Geraldine who deny their folk roots and those such as Claudia's mother who are much closer to their black identity. Organic and animal metaphors frequently suggest the transplanting of cultures and expose the fractures in the lives of the characters. For example, the way in which Maureen's green knee socks make her legs look like dandelion stems that have lost their heads as she runs from Claudia and Pecola emphasises how in pursuing white norms she has lost her head; that is the knowledge of herself and her ancestry as a black person. Helene's capitulation to white society in *Sula* is emphasised by her comparison to a stray dog that wags its tail at the very shop doorway from which it has been kicked (21). In the criticism of white society to be found in the black community's stories are examples of how African-American English often contains within itself a sense of worth which colonialism and racism have not been able to eradicate. Blue Jack's 'old-timey' story in *The Bluest Eye* of the headless corpse of a white woman, murdered by her husband, who returns from the swamp in which she has been buried to search for a comb, bumping into everything as she goes, is a satire on white women's preoccupation with their own image.

Racism's entrenchment in a pervasive, albeit occasionally fractured, power system is conveyed by the use of inanimate metaphors. For example, the white boys who threaten Sula and Nel are said to stand 'like a gate blocking the path' (*Sula*, 54). The men who force Cholly in *The Bluest Eye* to have intercourse with Darlene while they watch become inseparable from their lights; the leader, for example, is referred to as 'flashlight man'. The effect of this is to enhance not only the pervasiveness of their power with the flashlights as symbols of an intimidating surveillance, but also its anonymity. The beams represent the white men's vicarious penetration not only of Darlene but also of Cholly; the flashlight is transformed metaphorically into a worm that bores into him, encapsulating the effects of his psychological humiliation. In the course of the passage, the refrain of the white men's laughter becomes piercing and consistent like the beams from which they are ultimately inseparable (*The Bluest Eye*, 116). bell hooks (1992) has reminded us that:

> Socialized to believe the fantasy that whiteness represents goodness and all that is benign and non-threatening, many white people assume this is the way black people conceptualize whiteness. They do not imagine that the way whiteness makes its presence felt in black life, most often as terrorizing imposition, a power that wounds, hurts, tortures, is a reality that disrupts the fantasy of whiteness as representing goodness. (340–1)

Inanimate metaphors are also similarly used to describe the contempt towards their own race of blacks who assume the attitudes and values of the host society. The scorn which Pecola in *The Bluest Eye* has to endure is envisaged as a flow of volcanic lava consuming what lies in its path. Macon Dead's disappointment over his daughters in *Song of Solomon* 'sifted down on them like ash, dulling their buttery complexions and choking the lilt out of what should have been girlish voices' (10).

The vividness of Morrison's writing is attributable not only to its innovation but to its meticulousness, enhanced by the specificity of much of the observation. Cholly's powerlessness over his own body and his physical environment in the episode discussed above is emphasised in the detail of his eyes sliding around furtively for shelter. The juxtaposition of the paralysed body and moving eyes underlines how the humiliation of being caught by the white men alienates him from his own body and how his body, like that of many black people, has become a site of subjugation upon which others demonstrate their power over him. For many of the characters in Morrison's novels their bodies are sources not of celebration but constant anxiety; the visual representation of the identity for which, as black people, they are victimised. Many of the most poignant observations are embedded in how bodies are received by others or become focal points or are objects of encoding. Claudia in *The Bluest Eye* has noticed what she calls the 'slippery light' in the eyes of teachers when they are confronted with black students who aspire to white values and norms (57). The tension between Yacobowski and Pecola as a child is conveyed in his reluctance to touch her – the first time she is made aware of her body as the representation and site of her status as 'black' within a majority white society. His nails are said to graze her damp palms. The reference to 'nails' rather than 'finger nails' make them seem like claws while the dampness of her hands betrays the anxiety which is to be a permanent feature of her identity. The description of the nails scraping her palm is especially effective for it is the vulnerable, underside of the child's hands which they score. Morrison's work is made especially vivid by this attention to the nuances in communication between people. When Milkman returns from the hunting expedition in which he has proved himself to the Southern blacks in *Song of Solomon*, his excitement and euphoria are contained in his confessional, unguarded, childlike spontaneity while his new-found sense of camaraderie in the exchanges with the other hunters is conveyed through basic, childlike sentence structures: 'I dropped the gun. I tripped and it went off. Then when I picked it up it went off again' (280).

Space in the novels is, as Baker et al. contend, an 'imagistic field' in which objective reality and subjective experience co-exist (Baker and Redmond, 1989, 150). An examination of these fields reveals the values and beliefs which affect individual lives. For example, in *The Bluest Eye*, space differentiates, as Baker says of *Sula*, into a Euro-American space and an African-American space which can be differentiated further into gendered space. The sentences which describe the idealised Euro-American field are short, emphatic and certain, whilst those that delineate the Breedlove's home are less emphatic and less certain. The language reflects the nature of the Breedlove's home where rooms are only partitioned spaces, not solid and discernible areas. Even the colours are not the bright, bold ones of the American primer but are depressing and melancholy. However, Baker does not take the analysis far enough for the gendered space can be divided again in terms of class and race, as is evident from the different statuses accorded the families which constitute the black neighbourhood.

Through their distressing and often violent subject matter, Morrison's novels are frequently cathartic, as can be illustrated at the micro-level from *Beloved* where the trees are said to absorb the laughter of Sethe, Denver and Beloved as they skate on the ice, fighting 'gravity for each other's hands': 'Their skirts flew like wings and their skin turned pewter in the cold and dying light' (174). The language makes us aware of what has been temporarily exorcised – the horrors of the past – through the mention of trees which earlier in the novel reminded Sethe of the men hanged from them. Now the trees appear to participate in her and her children's joy while their uplfted spirits are described in a metaphor of escape. This passage is especially effective because of the way in which human contact and reassurance through touch facilitates transcendence of pain. Crucial to the cathartic aspects of the novels at the macro- and micro-levels are the ways in which they involve the reader as participant, evident, for example, at the end of *Jazz*; 'You are free to do it and I am free to let you because look, look. Look where your hands are. Now' (229). Or through the refrain at the end of *Beloved*: 'It was not a story to pass on' (274–5).

It is difficult to read Morrison's novels without being affected as much by the rhythm or music of the prose as by its content. Images of music pervade Morrison's works, many of her women characters – Poland, Claudia's mother, Pilate, Sethe, for example – rely on songs which, as Rigney (1990) argues, break 'an enforced silence' and are expressions of desire (9). In the last two pages of *Song of Solomon*, Milkman's song for Sugargirl and its echo from the hills serve to introduce a new musical element in the prose even at the last minute. *Tar Baby* concludes with Son running 'Lickety-split. Lickety-split' and so on. In *Beloved*, the rhythmic repetition of elements in the first lines of chapters helps to unite them like the squares of a quilt: 'Beloved, she my daughter. She mine' (200); 'Beloved is my sister' (205); 'I am Beloved and she is mine' (210); 'I am Beloved and she is mine' (214).

The involvement of the reader as a participant through the musical quality of the writing, however, is only one of a number of ways in which the novels achieve their catharsis. Rigney (1990) suggests that the novels also, and for her most importantly, achieve redemption through that which is erotic. Drawing on French theorists such as Hélène Cixous, she argues that Morrison's work 'writes the female body' through language that imitates and recreates feminine orgasm and erogenous zones (104). Certainly Morrison's language is often diffusely sensual and at times overtly euphoric as in Pauline's recollection of intense feminine orgasm. Eating in the novels, as Rigney (1990) convincingly demonstrates, is often expressive of *Jouissance* as may be illustrated by the watermelon which Cholly remembers in *The Bluest Eye*, the ice-cream in *Sula*, or the bright orange which Pilate eats in *Song of Solomon* (83–4). But the cathartic element in the novels relies not so much on the erotic alone, as on a blues-type movement back and forth, across and between a whole range of experiences. Eating may often be erotic in Morrison's works but food is also associated with pain and humiliation, such as the candy which Pecola purchases with an image of a blue-eyed blonde girl on the wrapping or the mother's milk in *Song of Solomon* and *Beloved*.

The language of Morrison's novels makes the strongest case of all for approaching them as innovative texts driven by their radical African-American content. Whilst there is much more than the space here allows to say about Morrison's language, the key elements are its vividness, its use of colour, its sensuality, the specificity of the observation, its metaphoric mode of enunciation, its folk creativity, its cathartic qualities, the rhythm and the music, and, above all, the way in which community memory is not accessed through but stored in the language.

9

Postscript

The original definitions of me as a Black writer were an attempt to reduce the area in which I wrote, to ghettoise me – I'm forceful so I turned that around as those are the sensibilities out of which I write. (Morrison in Kenyon, 1993, 12)

Toni Morrison has written more novels to date than any other African-American woman writer. There should be more – may be many more – to come. For the same reasons as Norman Page in his volume in this series on Muriel Spark, I have decided to provide a postscript rather than a conclusion. As Professor Page points out, 'claims of conclusiveness where the work of a living writer is concerned seem impertinent, if not fraudulent'. If it is inappropriate to provide a conclusion in discussing the work to date of a living and prolific writer, it is especially so in Morrison's case, however, for in her novels she always eschews closure as incompatible with the black artistic sensibility. As she observed in interview with McKay (1983): 'Jazz always keeps you on the edge. There is no final chord . . . a long chord, but no final chord' (429). There is, however, more consensus as to Morrison's status as a novelist than is the case with Muriel Spark, but as the debates which followed her award of the Nobel Prize revealed, she also courts more vehement controversy.

One controversial aspect of Morrison's work has been her delineation of the heterogeneous nature of the African-American community and her exposure of the violence and sexual abuse which black women and black children have suffered at the hands of some black men. Appreciation of these subjects in her novels has developed alongside shifts in critical approaches to African-American literature. McDowell

(Baker and Redmond, 1989) revising her earlier paper (McKay, 1988), suggests that two seminal articles have helped shape recent attitudes to black women's writing (56). The first of these, Carby (1985), has demonstrated that black women's writing can generate its own distinctive, critical discourses while Braxton (1986) has shown that the customary critical framework and paradigms need not be reflexively and habitually employed. These conventional approaches have tended to include an image-conscious criticism, in which race is the sole determinant of identity, subsuming sexual difference, and to presume that identity is pre-existent, coherent and knowable. Reclaiming female voices and narratives has always been one of Morrison's objectives in writing as she explains in an interview with Kenyon (1993):

> Well, in the sixties our principal interpreters were Black men. Of course their position is unassailable; but I have little in common with Wright and Ellison because there was a void at the centre, no female voice. I had the feeling they were not talking to me, their editorial address was explanatory, to other men, possibly to white men. I realise now I wanted an interior life, experienced by a woman, at a particular time. I was longing for something that didn't exist in their work. (14)

In Morrison's novels the communal 'we' is the site of internecine, internal struggles mediated, as we have seen in so many cases including Claudia, Sula, Jadine, Sethe, Violet, by multiple subjectivities. Categorisation and self-labelling, which are acknowledged as part of the process by which identities are developed, are seen primarily as agents of control, restriction or inhibition. Identities are not perceived as pre-given, automatic or fixed, but socially organised, contingent, changeable and relational.

The novels are concerned with people who in terms of their ancestry are displaced, dispossessed and separated from their identity and history. But there is strong recognition throughout the writings that this identity and history should not be seen as stable or essentialist. Boundaries and limits are perceived as signifying spaces in which cultural, political and economic power are contested, negotiated or reaffirmed. In some of the novels, *The Bluest Eye* and *Song of Solomon* for example, there is sympathy for the way in which the past, in the context of the instability and unpredictability of the present, becomes a locus for an imagined community, a fantasy of identity and belonging which turns on notions of origins, roots, unarticulated histories and shared heritages. But this always stands in contradistinction, especially in *Song of Solomon*, to suspicions about mythologising; if Solomon is a mythical hero, he is also a father who deserted his wife and children. There is no easy retreat, as Son discovers in *Tar Baby*, into ethnic absolutism or illusory notions of classless, organic community. *Tar Baby* particularly refocuses attention on the displaced person, the migrant and the stranger, as separated from their history and identity. Resisting, as we said above, seeing these concepts of history and identity, as fixed or essentialist, the novel predicates the identity of the displaced person – Son, Jadine, Valerian, Margaret, Sydney, Ondine – on a new social space, the product of a complex global economy, new forms of economic imperialism and transnational communication. In *The Bluest Eye*, *Sula* and *Tar Baby*, geopolitical boundaries at the local, national and, in the latter, international level are perceived as fluid, as sites of contested authority and power, which are in turn embroiled with internal crises of coherence and stability in African-American identity. However, the spatialised political aesthetic of the novels, evidenced in the imagistic fields to which we referred in the previous chapter, is only one dimension of their concern with identity although ultimately all are related. Throughout Morrison's work, to which the examples cited above are also testimony, identity is the product of psychic struggle. The self is perceived as perpetually in process, as we discussed in the chapter on *Sula*, and her novels frequently employ strategies, as Hoffman (1985) points out, for 'rupturing' coherence of character. Often it is the unconscious, a sphere of conflict between ideas, longings and desires, which disrupts consciousness through dreams, memories, neurotic symptoms or unpredictable, even perverse, behaviours, as in the different cases of Pecola and Pauline in *The Bluest Eye*, Sethe and Paul D in *Beloved*, Violet and Joe in *Jazz*, for example.

Often the innovatory nature of Morrison's work at the level of what Gérard Genette called 'récit' is a product of its 'relational perspective' that is, a perspective which tries to understand events and practices as aspects of wider, social relations in order to unravel the contexts in which they become meaningful. As we saw in the discussion of Cholly's rape of his daughter in *The Bluest Eye* and Sethe's murder of her child in *Beloved*, this involves understanding the power relations at play and the cohesive limits which are placed on choice for black people. It also necessitates reclaiming Morrison from what Wallace (1992) describes as 'a newly depoliticised, mainstreamed, and commodified black feminist literary criticism' (661). She argues that critics, such as Gates, Jr, have failed to portray African-American writing 'as a "minority" literature hotly engaged in an antagonistic dialogue with a majority "white culture" in order to transcend and/or transform it' (660). It is important to recognise how often in Morrison's work we are challenged, for example in Sethe's case, to rethink the criteria by which we decide between appropriate and inappropriate behaviours. We have discussed in a previous chapter how the narrative of *Sula* forces us to question our readings, to hold our judgements in check and frequently to revise them. Indeed, as McDowell points, out, *Sula* employs time-breaks which compel the reader to pause, reflect and evaluate the narrative's events (Baker and Redmond, 1989, 68). As readers we have to learn what Son has to glean in his relationship with Jadine, that we can only make and judge choices by fully understanding their social and political contexts. Son's struggle against the oppressiveness of race while colluding in gender oppression epitomises his failure to understand fully how power operates through a web of interlocking practices. But Son also illustrates how challenges to oppressive forms are not only complex but often contradictory. New politics of sexuality and race create new spaces but also open up new fissures, creating new hostilities. The critique of black essentialism which to some extent underpins all of Morrison's work casts light in the novels on hidden but controlling assumptions and opens up new questions about history, power, meaning, diversity and choice. Ultimately all Morrison's novels are anchored in an ever growing social complexity; the new pluralism of racial, ethnic, class and cultural forms. Many of the novels, for example, *Song of Solomon*, *Sula* and *Tar Baby*, search for a collective way of dealing with differentiated identities, themselves the products of racial, gender and geographical differences.

In the early novels there is clear evidence of the influence of 1960s feminism with its stress on masculinised sexual codes perpetuating female oppression. But this perspective is developed by more emphasis being placed on the politics of female desire. Without foregoing issues around power, violence, victimisation and exploitation – explored in Pauline's relationship with Cholly, for example – the possibilities of sexual freedom and questions of pleasure and personal autonomy are pursued, for instance, in the cases of Sula and First Corinthians in *Song of Solomon*, Jadine in *Tar Baby* and Joe in *Jazz*. Yet sexual expression can only become an act of self-exploration where an individual is not 'fixed' on one locatable ego (McDowell in Baker and Redmond, 1989, 64–5).

This is clearly evident in the case of Macon Dead in *Song of Solomon* and, in a different way, it becomes Sula's problem also.

In order to be fully resistant to approaching African-American women's writing through a depoliticised, mainstreamed, and commodified literary criticism, it would be necessary to pursue some difficult questions. The publication of black writers to academic acclaim and their critical success in conferences, in journals and in colleges dominated by white Europeans must contribute to ongoing debates. These should include: ways in which their work calls into question academic notions of canonical literary traditions; the elitist nature of the avant-garde; and the consistency of their work with the tastes of the majority of black people. Issues such as these would require a book three times as long as this study to even begin to do them justice.

Within the limitations of the space available, this study has tried to bear in mind the potential impact of Morrison's work on how racism and sexism are perceived in contemporary culture. It has tried to show that Morrison's novels cannot be fully understood within the parameters of Euro-American literary criticism alone. Whilst bearing in mind the overall development of Morrison's work, the discussions of the individual novels have sought to demonstrate how each generates its own critical discourse. The experiment with form in all her novels derives from their radical content which includes the perception of boundaries and limits as spaces in which cultural, political and economic power are contested; resistance to retreat into illusory notions of community or ethnic absolutism; internecine, internal struggles in African-American identities mediated by multiple subjectivities. Morrison's novels give expression to voices, narratives and experiences which have not been previously articulated in the form of a novel. It is more fruitful to approach them from the perspective of how they pursue narrative possibilities which have not been previously developed in African-American and Euro-American fiction than from how they invert Euro-American literary conventions.

Select Bibliography

Awkward, Michael, 'Roadblocks and Relatives: Critical Revision in Toni Morrison's *The Bluest Eye*', in McKay, Nellie (ed.), *Critical Essays on Toni Morrison* (Boston: G. K. Hall, 1988).

Baker, Jr, Houston A., *Blues, Ideology and Afro-American Literature: A Theory of Literature* (Chicago: Chicago University Press, 1984).

Baker, Jr, Houston A. and Redmond, Patricia A. (eds), *Afro-American Literary Study in the 1990s* (Chicago: Chicago University Press, 1989).

Bakerman, Jane S., 'Failures of Love: Female Initiation in the novels of Toni Morrison', *American Literature*, 52 (1981), 541–63.

Bakhtin, M. M., *The Dialogic Imagination*, ed. Holquist, Michael, trs. Emerson, Caryl and Holquist, Michael (1975) (Austin: University of Texas Press, 1981).

Barthes, Roland, 'Theory of the Text', tr. Ian McLeod, in Young, Robert (ed.), *Untying the Text: a Post-structuralist Reader* (London: Routledge, 1981).

Barthold, Bonnie, *Black Time: Fiction of Africa, the Caribbean, and the United States* (New Haven: Yale University Press, 1981).

Bhabha, Homi K., *The Location of Culture* (London: Routledge, 1994).

Bigsby, Christopher, *The Second Black Renaissance: Essays in Black Literature* (London: Greenwood Press, 1980).

Bigsby, Christopher, 'Jazz Queen', *The Independent*, 26 April 1992, 28–9.

Bloom, Harold (ed.), *Modern Critical Views: Toni Morrison* (New York: Chelsea House, 1990).

Bradbury, Malcolm and Palmer, David (eds), *The American Novel in the Nineteen Twenties* (London: Arnold, 1971).

Braxton, Joanne M., 'Harriet Jacobs' *Incidents in the Life of a Slave Girl*', *Massachusetts Review*, 27 (1986), 380–1.

Braxton, Joanne M. and McLaughlin, Andrée Nicola, *Wild Women in the Whirlwind: Afra-American Culture and the Contemporary Literary Renaissance* (London: Serpent's Tail, 1990).

Butler-Evans, Elliott, *Race, Gender and Desire: Narrative Strategies in the Fiction of Toni Cade Bambara, Toni Morrison and Alice Walker* (Philadelphia: Temple University Press, 1989).

Carby, Hazel, ' "On the threshold of Woman's Era": Lynchings, Empire and Sexuality in Black Feminist Theory', *Critical Inquiry*, 12 (1985), 263.

Christian, Barbara, 'Community and Nature in the Novels of Toni Morrison', *Journal of Ethnic Studies*, 7 (Winter 1980), 64–78.

Christian, Barbara, *Black Feminist Criticism: Perspectives on Black Women Writers* (New York: Pergamon Press, 1985).

Clarke, Graham (ed.), *The New American Writing: Essays on American Literature since 1970* (London: Vision Press, 1990).

Coward, Rosalind, *Female Desire* (London: Paladin Books, 1984 rpt. 1985).

Davies, Cynthia A., 'Self, Society, and Myth in Toni Morrison's Fiction', *Contemporary Literature*, 23 (1982), 323–42.

de Weever, Jacqueline, *Mythmaking and Metaphor in Black Women's Fiction* (New York: St. Martin's Press, 1991).

Derrida, Jacques, *Marges de la Philosophie*, tr. Alan Bass (Chicago: Chicago University Press, 1982).

Derrida, Jacques, *La Carte Postale*, tr. Alan Bass (Chicago; Chicago University Press, 1987).

Evans, Mari (ed.), *Black Women Writers (1950–1980): a Critical Evaluation* (New York: Anchor Books, 1984).

Fabre, Genevieve, 'Genealogical Archaeology or the Quest for Legacy in Toni Morrison's *Song of Solomon*', in McKay, Nellie (ed.), *Critical Essays on Toni Morrison* (Boston: G. H. Hall, 1988).

Gates, Jr, Henry Louis (ed.), *Black Literature and Literary Theory* (London: Routledge, 1984).

Gates, Jr, Henry Louis (ed.), *'Race', Writing, and Difference* (Chicago: University of Chicago Press, 1985).

Gates, Jr, Henry Louis, *Loose Canons: Notes on the Culture Wars* (London: Oxford University Press, 1992).

Genette, Gérard, *Narrative Discourse: An Essay in Method* (1972), tr. Jane E. Lewin (Ithaca: Cornell University Press, 1980).

Gibson, Andrew, *Reading Narrative Discourse: Studies in the Novel from Cervantes to Beckett* (London: Macmillan, 1990).

Gikandi, Simon, *Reading the African Novel* (London: Curry, 1987).

Gilroy, Paul, *Small Acts: Thoughts on the Politics of Black Cultures* (London: Serpent's Tail, 1993).

Grant, Robert, 'Absence into Presence: The Thematics of Memory and "Missing" Subjects in Toni Morrison's *Sula*', in McKay, Nellie (ed.), *Critical Essays on Toni Morrison* (Boston: G. K. Hall, 1988).

Grossberg, Lawrence, Nelson, Cary and Treichler, Paula, *Cultural Studies* (London: Routledge, 1992).

Harper, Michael S. and Stepto, Robert B., *Chant of Saints* (Urbana: University of Illinois Press, 1979).

Harris, Trudier, 'Reconnecting Fragments: Afro-American Folk Tradition in *The Bluest Eye*', in McKay, Nellie (ed.), *Critical Essays on Toni Morrison* (Boston: G. K. Hall, 1988).

Hoffman, Baruch, *Character in Literature* (Ithaca: Cornell University Press, 1985).

hooks, bell, 'Representing Whiteness in the Black Imagination' in Grossberg et al., *Cultural Studies* (London: Routledge, 1992).

House, Elizabeth B., 'Artists and the Art of Living: Order and Disorder in Toni Morrison's Fiction', *Modern Fiction Studies*, 34 (1988), 27–44.

Hughes, Langston, *The Big Sea* (New York: Thunder's Mouth Press, 1986).

Hull, Gloria T., Scott, Patricia Bell and Smith, Barbara (eds), *All the Women Are White, All the Blacks Are Men, But Some of Us Are Brave: Black Women's Studies* (Old Westbury, New York: Feminist Press, 1982).

Jaye, Michael C. and Watts, Ann C. (eds), *Literature and the American Urban Experience: Essays on the City and Literature* (Manchester: Manchester University Press, 1981).

Keith, Michael and Pile, Steve, *Place and the Politics of Identity* (London: Routledge, 1993).

Kenyon, Olga, *Writing Women: Contemporary Women Novelists* (London: Pluto Press, 1991).

Kenyon, Olga, 'Interview with Toni Morrison', *Baetyl*, 2 (1993), 11–23.

Kenyon, Olga, ' "Writing as a Black Woman Makes My World Larger": the writings of Toni Morrison', *Baetyl*, 2 (1993), 24–46.

Krumholz, Linda, 'Dead Teachers: Rituals of Manhood and Rituals of Reading in *Song of Solomon*', *Modern Fiction Studies*, 39 (1993), 551–74.

LeClair, Thomas, 'The Language must not Sweat: A Conversation with Toni Morrison', *New Republic*, 21 March 1981.

Lee, Dorothy H., 'Song of Solomon: to Ride the Air', *Black American Literature Forum*, 16 (1982), 64–70.

Lester, Rosemarie K., 'An interview with Toni Morrison', in McKay, Nellie (ed.), *Critical Essays on Toni Morrison* (Boston: G. K. Hall, 1988).

Lewis, Peter, 'Making Magic', *The Independent*, 3 April 1993, 24–6.

Lowmax, L. E., *The Negro Revolt* (London: Hamish Hamilton, 1962).

Mbalia, Doreatha Drummond, 'Women Who Run With Wild: the Need for Sisterhoods in *Jazz*', *Modern Fiction Studies*, 39 (1993), 623–4.

Mbalia, Doreatha Drummond, *Toni Morrison's Developing Class Consciousness* (London: Associated University Presses, 1991).

McDowell, Deborah, ' "The Self and Other": Reading Toni Morrison's *Sula* and the Black Female Text', in McKay, Nellie (ed.), *Critical Essays on Toni Morrison* (Boston: G. K. Hall, 1988).

McDowell, Deborah, 'Boundaries: or Distant Relations and Close Kin', in Baker, Jr, Houston A. and Redmond, Patricia A. (eds), *Afro-American Literary Study in the 1990s* (Chicago: Chicago University Press, 1989).

McKay, Nellie, 'An Interview with Toni Morrison', *Contemporary Literature*, 24 (1983), 411–29.

McKay, Nellie (ed.), *Critical Essays on Toni Morrison* (Boston: G. K. Hall, 1988).

Milford, Nancy, *Zelda* (New York: Avon Books, 1971).

Mix, Debbie, 'Toni Morrison: a Selected Bibliography', *Modern Fiction Studies*, 39 (1993), 795–817.

Mobley, Marilyn Sanders, 'A Different Remembering: Memory, History and Meaning in Toni Morrison's *Beloved*' in Bloom, Harold (ed.), *Modern Critical Views: Toni Morrison* (New York: Chelsea House, 1990).

Morrison, Toni, 'City Limits, Village Values: Concepts of the Neighbourhood in Black Fiction' in Jayne, Michael C. and Watts, Ann C. (eds), *Literature and the American Urban Experience: Essays on the City and Literature* (Manchester: Manchester University Press, 1981).

Morrison, Toni, 'Rootedness: The Ancestor as Foundation' in Evans, Mari (ed.), *Black Women Writers (1950–1980): a Critical Evaluation* (New York:

Anchor Books, 1984). Also in Walder, Dennis (ed.), *Literature in the Modern World: Critical Essays and Documents* (London: Oxford University Press, 1990).

Morrison, Toni, *Playing in the Dark* (Cambridge, Mass.: Harvard University Press, 1992).

Morrison, Toni, *Race-ing Justice, En-gendering Power* (London: Chatto & Windus, 1993).

Nasta, Susheila (ed.), *Motherlands: Black Women's Writing from Africa, the Caribbean and South Asia* (London: The Women's Press, 1991).

Oakley, Giles, *The Devil's Music: A History of the Blues* (London: British Broadcasting Corporation, 1976).

Otten, Terry, *The Crime of Innocence in the Fiction of Toni Morrison* (Columbia, University of Missouri Press, 1989).

Pérez-Torres, Rafael, 'Knitting and Knotting the Narrative Thread – *Beloved* as a Postmodern Novel', *Modern Fiction Studies*, 39 (1993), 689–707.

Piersen, William D., *Black Legacy: America's Hidden Heritage* (Boston: University of Massachusetts Press, 1994).

Radin, Paul, *The Trickster* (London: Routledge, 1956).

Rice, Alan, 'Take It From The Top', *The Times Higher Education Supplement*, 19 June 1992, 16.

Rigney, Barbara Hill, *The Voices of Toni Morrison* (Columbus: Ohio State University Press, 1991).

Rodrigues, Eusebio L., 'Experiencing *Jazz*', *Modern Fiction Studies*, 39 (1993), 733–54.

Rushdy, Ashraf H. A., ' "Rememory": Primal Scenes and Constructions in Toni Morrison's Novels', *Contemporary Literature*, 31 (1990), 300–23.

Ryan, Judylyn S., 'Contested Visions/Double-Vision in *Tar Baby*', *Modern Fiction Studies*, 39, (1993), 597–621.

Samuels, Wilfred D. and Hudson-Weems, Clenora, *Toni Morrison* (Boston: Twayne Publishers, 1990).

Segy, Ladistas, *Masks of Black Africa* (New York: Dover Publications, 1976).

Shaw, Arnold, *The Jazz Age* (London: Oxford University Press, 1987).

Showalter, E. (ed.), *The New Feminist Criticism: Essays on Women, Literature and Theory* (London: Virago, 1986).

Selmon, Stephen, 'Magic Realism as Post-Colonial Discourse', *Canadian Literature*, 116 (1989), 9–24.

Smith, Valerie, *Self-Discovery and Authority in Afro-American Narrative* (Cambridge, Mass.: Harvard University Press, 1987).

Soja, Edward W., *Postmodern Geographies: the Reassertion of Space in Critical Social Theory* (London: Verso, 1989).

Tate, Claudia (ed.), *Black Women Writers at Work* (Harpenden: Oldcastle Books, 1985).

Tate, Claudia, 'On Black Literary Women and the Evolution of Critical Discourse', *Tulsa Studies in Women's Literature*, 5 (1986), 111–23.

Traylor, Eleanor W., 'The Fabulous World of Toni Morrison: *Tar Baby*', in McKay, Nellie (ed.), *Critical Essays on Toni Morrison* (Boston: G. K. Hall, 1988).

Walder, Dennis, *Literature in the Modern World: Critical Essays and Documents* (London: Oxford University Press, 1990).

Walker, Melissa, *Black Women's Novels in the Wake of the Civil Rights Movement, 1966–1989* (London and New Haven: Yale University Press, 1991).

Walker, Nancy, 'Reformers and Young Maidens: Women and Virtue', in Bloom, Harold (ed.), *Mark Twain's Adventures of Huckleberry Finn: Modern Critical Interpretations* (New York: Chelsea House Publishers, 1986).

Wallace, Michelle, 'Towards A Black Feminist Cultural Criticism', in Grossberg, Lawrence et al., *Cultural Studies* (London: Routledge, 1992).

Werner, Craig H., 'The Briar Patch as Modernist Myth: Morrison, Barthes and *Tar Baby* As-Is', in McKay, Nellie (ed.), *Critical Essays on Toni Morrison* (G. K. Hall, 1988).

Wilentz, Gay, *Binding Cultures: Black Women Writers in Africa and the Diaspora* (Bloomington and Indianapolis: Indiana University Press, 1992).

Wilkerson, Margaret B., 'The Dramatic Voice in Toni Morrison's Novels', in McKay, Nellie (ed.), *Critical Essays on Toni Morrison* (Boston: G. K. Hall, 1988).

Wisker, Gina (ed.), *Black Women's Writing* (London: Macmillan, 1993).

Index